Letters to the Ephesians and Timothy

GUIDANCE FOR THE CHURCH AND ITS LEADERS

JOE BLAIR
DAVID MORGAN
ALLEN REASONS
FELISI SORGWE
BILL TILLMAN
FRANCE BROWN
JANET BURTON
EMILY MARTIN
TRACI POE

BAPTISTWAYPRESS®

Dallas, Texas

*Letters to the Ephesians and Timothy: Guidance for the Church
and Its Leaders—Adult Bible Teaching Guide*

BAPTISTWAY PRESS® Leadership Team
Executive Director, Baptist General Convention of Texas: David Hardage
Director, Church Ministry Resources: Chris Liebrum
Director, Bible Study/Discipleship Team: Phil Miller
Publisher, BaptistWay Press®: Scott Stevens

Publishing consultant and editor: Ross West
Cover and Interior Design and Production: Desktop Miracles, Inc.
Printing: Data Reproductions Corporation

First edition: September 2014
ISBN–13: 978–1–938355–24–0

How to Make the Best Use of *This* Teaching Guide

Leading a class in studying the Bible is a sacred trust. This *Teaching Guide* has been prepared to help you as you give your best to this important task.

In each lesson, you will find first "Bible Comments" for teachers, to aid you in your study and preparation. The three sections of "Bible Comments" are "Understanding the Context," "Interpreting the Scriptures," and "Focusing on the Meaning." "Understanding the Context" provides a summary overview of the entire background passage that also sets the passage in the context of the Bible book being studied. "Interpreting the Scriptures" provides verse-by-verse comments on the focal passage. "Focusing on the Meaning" offers help with the meaning and application of the focal text.

The second main part of each lesson is "Teaching Plans." You'll find two complete teaching plans in this section. The first is called "Teaching Plan—Varied Learning Activities," and the second is called "Teaching Plan—Lecture and Questions." Choose the plan that best fits your class and your style of teaching. You may also use and adapt ideas from both. Each plan is intended to be practical, helpful, and immediately useful as you prepare to teach.

The major headings in each teaching plan are intended to help you sequence how you teach so as to follow the flow of how people tend to learn. The first major heading, "Connect with Life," provides ideas that will help you begin the class session where your class is and draw your class into the study. The second major heading, "Guide Bible Study," offers suggestions for helping your class engage the Scriptures actively and develop a greater understanding of this portion of the Bible's message. The third major heading, "Encourage Application," is meant to help participants focus on how to respond with their lives to this message.

As you begin the study with your class, be sure to find a way to help your class know the date on which each lesson will be studied. You might use one or more of the following methods:

- In the first session of the study, briefly overview the study by identifying with your class the date on which each lesson will be studied. Lead your class to write the date in the table of contents in their *Study Guides* and on the first page of each lesson.
- Make and post a chart that indicates the date on which each lesson will be studied.
- If all of your class has e-mail, send them an e-mail with the dates the lessons will be studied.
- Provide a bookmark with the lesson dates. You may want to include information about your church and then use the bookmark as an outreach tool, too. A model for a bookmark can be downloaded from www.baptistwaypress.org on the Resources for Adults page.
- Develop a sticker with the lesson dates, and place it on the table of contents or on the back cover.

Here are some steps you can take to help you prepare well to teach each lesson and save time in doing so:

1. Start early in the week before your class meets.

2. If your church's adult Bible study teachers meet for lesson overview and preparation, plan to participate. If your church's adult Bible study teachers don't have this planning time now, look for ways to begin. You, your fellow teachers, and your church will benefit from this mutual encouragement and preparation.

3. Overview the study in the *Study Guide*. Look at the table of contents, and see where this lesson fits in the overall study. Then read or review the study introduction to the book that is being studied.

4. Consider carefully the suggested Main Idea, Question to Explore, and Teaching Aim. These can help you discover the main thrust of this particular lesson.

5. Use your Bible to read and consider prayerfully the Scripture passages for the lesson. Using your Bible in your study and in the class session can provide a positive model to class members to use their

own Bibles and give more attention to Bible study themselves. (Each writer of the Bible comments in both the *Teaching Guide* and the *Study Guide* has chosen a favorite translation. You're free to use the Bible translation you prefer and compare it with the translations chosen, of course.)

6. After reading all the Scripture passages in your Bible, then read the Bible comments in the *Study Guide.* The Bible comments are intended to be an aid to your study of the Bible. Read also the small articles—"sidebars"—in each lesson. They are intended to provide additional, enrichment information and inspiration and to encourage thought and application. Try to answer for yourself the questions included in each lesson. They're intended to encourage further thought and application, and you can also use them in the class session itself. Continue your Bible study with the aid of the Bible comments included in this *Teaching Guide.*

7. Review the "Teaching Plans" in this *Teaching Guide.* Consider how these suggestions would help you teach this Bible passage in your class to accomplish the teaching aim.

8. Consider prayerfully the needs of your class, and think about how to teach so you can help your class learn best.

9. Develop and follow a lesson plan based on the suggestions in this *Teaching Guide,* with alterations as needed for your class.

10. Enjoy leading your class in discovering the meaning of the Scripture passages and in applying these passages to their lives.

Adult Online Bible Commentary. Plan to get the additional adult Bible study comments available online. Call 1–866–249–1799 or e-mail baptistway@texasbaptists.org to order *Adult Online Bible Commentary.* It is available only in electronic format (PDF) from our website. The price of these comments is $6 for individuals and $25 for a group of five. A church or class that participates in our advance order program for free shipping can receive *Adult Online Bible Commentary* free. Call 1–866–249–1799 or see www.baptistwaypress.org for information on participating in our free shipping program for the next study.

Adult Online Teaching Plans. An additional teaching plan is also available in electronic format (PDF) by calling 1–866–249–1799. The price of these plans for an entire study is $5 for an individual **or** $20 for a group of five. It is available only in electronic format (PDF) from our website. A church or class that participates in our advance order program for free shipping can receive *Adult Online Teaching Plans* free. Call 1–866–249–1799 or see www.baptistwaypress.org for information on participating in our free shipping program for the next study.

FREE! Downloadable teaching resource items for use in your class are available at www.baptistwaypress.org! Watch for them in "Teaching Plans" for each lesson. Then go online to www.baptistwaypress.org and click on "Teaching Resource Items" for this study. These items are selected from "Teaching Plans." They are provided online to make lesson preparation easier for hand-outs and similar items. Permission is granted to download these teaching resource items, print them out, copy them as needed, and use them in your class.

IN ADDITION: Enrichment teaching help is provided in the online *Baptist Standard,* which is available at www.baptiststandard.com. The *Baptist Standard* is available online for an annual subscription rate of $10. Subscribe online at www.baptiststandard.com or call 214–630–4571. A free ninety-day trial subscription is currently available.

Writers of This Teaching Guide

David Morgan wrote **"Bible Comments" on lessons one and two.** He is pastor of the Trinity Baptist Church, Harker Heights, Texas. He is a graduate of Hardin-Simmons University (B.A.) and of Southwestern Baptist Theological Seminary (M.Div., Ph.D.). Dr. Morgan also serves as an adjunct professor at the University of Mary Hardin-Baylor, Belton, Texas.

Bill Tillman, writer of **"Bible Comments" for lessons three and four,** is director of Theological Education for Texas Baptists. Dr. Tillman previously served as T.B. Maston Professor of Christian Ethics, Logsdon School of Theology, Hardin-Simmons University. He is a member of First Baptist Church, Abilene, Texas.

Emily Martin wrote **"Teaching Plans" for lessons one through four.** She is a professional writer specializing in business and Christian communication. She and her husband have a son and a daughter and are members of Park Cities Baptist Church, Dallas, Texas. She has written numerous teaching plans for BaptistWay Press®.

Allen Reasons, writer of **"Bible Comments" for lessons five through seven,** is the senior minister of Fifth Avenue Baptist Church, Huntington, West Virginia. He also serves as an adjunct professor for Palmer Theological Seminary. He has previously served as pastor of churches in Texas and Missouri. Dr. Reasons holds the Doctor of Philosophy degree from Southwestern Baptist Theological Seminary. He and his wife Lauri have two children, Katherine and Preston. Katherine is married to Eric Pyles, and they have one child, James.

France Brown wrote **"Teaching Plans" for lessons five through seven.** He serves as the Ernest L. Mays Assistant Professor of Expository Preaching & Biblical Teaching at the College of Biblical Studies— Houston. He is the author of two books: *Passport to Life: Explore God's*

Word, Experience God's Blessings and *Transformational Teaching: A guide to developing and delivering life changing Bible lessons.* France gives leadership to the Christian education ministry at the New Providence Baptist Church, Houston, Texas. He is a graduate of Blinn College (A.A.), Texas A&M University (B.A.), and Dallas Theological Seminary (Th.M.).

Joe Blair wrote **"Bible Comments" for lessons eight through eleven.** Dr. Blair is professor of Christianity and Philosophy at Houston Baptist University, Houston, Texas. He has also taught at Union University, Jackson, Tennessee, and served as pastor of churches in Louisiana. He is a graduate of Louisiana Tech University and of New Orleans Baptist Theological Seminary (Th.D.).

Janet Burton, writer of "Teaching Plans" for lessons eight through eleven, is a pastor's wife, author, and Christian educator. She and her husband, Jack Burton, live in Austin, Texas, where they serve SkyView Baptist Church. The Burtons are parents of two grown sons. Janet has published two recent books for women: *A Touch of Jesus* and *Empowered Women.* She has written many teaching plans for BaptistWay Press®.

Felisi Sorgwe, writer of **"Bible Comments" for lessons twelve and thirteen,** is associate professor of Theology and director of the Center for Exploring Ministry Careers in the Department of Theology at Houston Baptist University, Houston, Texas. Dr. Sorgwe is also pastor of Maranatha International Church, Houston. A dual citizen of Nigeria and the United States, he received the M.Div. and M.A.R.E. degrees from Southwestern Baptist Theological Seminary and the Ph.D. in Religion degree from Baylor University.

Traci Poe wrote **"Teaching Plans" for lessons twelve and thirteen.** She is a leader in the children's, youth, and worship ministries at her home church, South Oaks Baptist Church, Arlington, Texas. She has a master's degree in Communication from the University of Denver and teaches communication and speech courses at a local university. Traci lives with her husband and their five children in Mansfield, Texas.

Letters to the Ephesians and Timothy: Guidance for the Church and Its Leaders

MAIN IDEA
God has lavishly and graciously provided salvation through Christ, who is Lord over all.

QUESTION TO EXPLORE
Why do we sometimes think of church as mere duty and obligation—or optional—when God has so lavishly provided salvation for us?

TEACHING AIM
To lead adults to describe God's lavish provisions of salvation through Christ

LESSON ONE
God's Lavish Provisions

BIBLE COMMENTS

Understanding the Context

Recent stories in my local newspaper covered sexual harassment in the armed forces, the future of the United States military in Afghanistan, the increase of car thefts in our community, and the lack of progress in the United States Congress to address immigration. While the specific stories may have changed by the time you read this, I suspect they will be similar. The situation appears overwhelming. What ought we to do? Is there any hope?

How Christians ought to live in a non-Christian world is the subject matter of Ephesians 4—6. Before Paul offered guidance on this subject, though, he first established a doctrinal foundation in chapters 1—3. What God has done for people in Christ precedes how God expects Christians to live.

In Ephesians 1:1, Paul introduced himself to his readers as God's authoritative representative. He also described his readers as holy and faithful followers of Christ.

Ephesians 1:3–23 consists of two major sections. The first section (1:3–14) shows what God has accomplished for believers in Christ and praises God because God had blessed them with every spiritual blessing. The blessings include a permanent salvation, which is characterized both as redemption and as forgiveness of sin. God had adopted Christians as children and sealed them with the Holy Spirit. Paul described God's free and enduring salvation that enabled Christians to live righteous and holy lives.

The second section (1:15–23) is a prayer for the readers of the letter. Paul offered regular thanks to God for his Christian readers. He prayed that God might continue to grant them growth in their Christian lives. He reminded them of the hope that was theirs in Christ and of the power of God. God had vested Christ, who was seated at God's right hand, with this power. God's people may face struggles as they attempt to live godly lives, but God's power is sufficient to give them success.[1]

Interpreting the Scriptures

From Apostle to Saints (1:1–2)

The opening of modern letters may be mere formality, but such was not true in Paul's day. Secular letters in his day offered more than the contemporary, *hey,* or *dear.* . . . The letters in the New Testament are even more detailed as the writers usually offered a personal introduction and a spiritual description of the readers as well.

1:1a. Paul described himself as an "apostle," that is, one sent on a mission by and with the authority of another. Paul wrote with the authority of Christ, and he expected his readers to heed his instructions. The phrase, "will of God," reveals that Paul recognized that both his salvation and his role as God's messenger were God's plan for him.

1:1b–2. Paul identified his readers as "saints" who were "faithful in Christ Jesus." But both the words for "saints" (literally *holy)* and "faithful" are adjectives. One possible way to understand Paul's description of the recipients is that they were *holy and faithful in Christ Jesus.* This expression emphasizes the character of the recipients more than their identity. It also reads smoothly in the Greek since, as is mentioned in "Studying *Letters to the Ephesians and Timothy: Guidance for the Church and Its Leaders*" in the *Adult Bible Study Guide,* the words, "in Ephesus," are missing from the best manuscripts.

The apostle blessed the readers by wishing for them "grace" and "peace." Peace can be linked to the Old Testament idea of *shalom. Shalom* not only suggests absence of conflict but also wholeness and well-being. In many ways, it is synonymous with salvation.

Spiritual Blessings in Christ (1:3–14)

1:3. The word "blessed," stresses that God alone is worthy of human worship. God has granted all kinds of spiritual gifts to Christians, not simply the gift of conversion. That the blessings do not come from this world is highlighted by the use of the phrase, "in the heavenly places." What God had accomplished in the heavens in Christ impacts the world through the lives of Christians. This spiritual transformation comes through the work of Christ ("in Christ").

1:4. The first specific aspect of the spiritual blessings is God's intentionally choosing of persons. The emphasis falls not on who is or is not chosen but on God's sovereignty and the assurance of God's power to accomplish God's will in their lives. Even more specifically, God chose us not simply to experience salvation but to live righteous and pure lives.

1:5–6. A second part of the blessing and part of being chosen is God's desire to bring us into God's family as adopted children. God has predestined salvation for those who will receive it. Christians derive a new identity from being God's children as well as from becoming heirs to divine blessings and power.

Three times in this passage we find words that express praise to God's grace ("glorious grace," 1:6; "glory," 1:12, 14). The glory of God is the revelation of God's nature. Once again, Paul declared God's graciousness. God has given Christians this gift through the work of Christ, the "Beloved."

1:7–8a. Another facet of the blessings Christians receive at conversion and still possess is "redemption," that is, *release or freedom from sin.* "Forgiveness" comes from a word that indicates that something, in this case sin, is sent away. Sin can mean either a falling away from the right way or the acts that result from separation from God. The word "trespasses" points to the latter in this verse. God's grace is more than sufficient ("lavished") to offer forgiveness.

1:8b–10. Another part of the Christian's blessing in Christ is God's revelation of the divine plan to bring all things together in Christ. "Mystery" refers not to something hidden but something once hidden that is now made known. The plan is that God will bring history to the end that God chose. At the appropriate time ("fullness of time"), God will fulfill and finalize the work through the power of Christ.

1:11–12. Both Jews and Gentiles are recipients of God's spiritual blessings. In verse 12, Paul distinguished between them, identifying Jews as "the first to set our hope on Christ." Jews were the original recipients of God's blessing.

1:13–14. These verses focus on the Gentiles' ("you also") acceptance of the salvation God offered. Paul's purpose was not so much to differentiate between the groups but to highlight to Gentiles first and then to Jewish Christians that the Gentiles were now part of God's adopted family. Gentiles had heard the good news ("gospel"). Paul clarified that hearing alone was not sufficient but that the Gentiles had also *believed* in Christ. That they "were marked with the seal" may refer to water baptism as the sign of their conversion. More importantly it signified that the Gentiles were protected by the authority and power of the Holy Spirit.

Paul described the Spirit as the "pledge" of the inheritance. The "seal of the promised Holy Spirit" was a deposit on a greater inheritance that they would receive. What they had received in Christ was only a foretaste of what lay ahead for them.

Paul's Prayer for His Readers (1:15–23)

In the second section of Ephesians 1:3–23, Paul thanked God for the faith and love of the saints. Paul's prayer unfolded his understanding of God's power at work among the faithful and the assurance that they would derive from the promise of that power.

1:15–16. "Faith" means two things in this verse. It means holding correct doctrine. We use it in this way when we refer to the content of our faith. The word also indicates the means by which people become members of the community of Christians. Paul mentioned "love" here as well as faith. They directed their "love toward all the saints" (*holy ones*). Paul reminded his readers of his regular prayers for them.

1:17. Paul, even as he prayed for his readers, assumed they would be maturing as Christians. Their growth might be marked with potholes and detours, but because of their commitment to Christ, they would be journeying in the right direction. While their participation was required, God would make growth possible. Paul prayed that they might receive God's "wisdom and revelation." The apostle believed God would guide the community of Christians and each Christian in their pilgrimage. The word "spirit" here refers to the human spirit that is being transformed in Christ.

1:18–19. Three images provide the reason Paul sought wisdom and revelation for the saints: (1) "the hope" to which God had called them; (2) "the riches of his glorious inheritance"; and (3) "the immeasurable greatness of his power." Each is associated with an "enlightened" heart. "Heart" describes not the place of emotions but the center of knowledge and the will. The imagery highlights one's spiritual formation. The word "hope" expresses confidence in God, not wishful thinking. The saints could live with an expectation that God would preserve them into their future. Paul longed for the believers to know God's riches, that is, to be aware of all the resources they had in God. Finally, Paul wanted them to know the magnitude of God's power. It was overflowing and abundant. They could withstand any trial, tribulation, or temptation because of God's enormous power. The second part of verse 19, "according to the working of his great power," adds further emphasis to God's strength.

1:20–21. The power that is available to Christians is the same power by which God resurrected Christ and placed him at God's right hand. Being seated at God's right hand, often considered the strongest hand, is a common symbol of power and authority. God has subjected all powers and institutions to Christ's authority. Christ is Lord over all things, in this age and in the age to come.

1:22–23. God has made Christ supreme ruler and "head over all things for the church." Paul added that the church is Christ's "body." Through it, Christ impacts the world. The church is the fullness of Christ's body as it continues and completes Christ's ministry in our world.

Focusing on the Meaning

God has blessed us as Christians with every spiritual blessing. Salvation (*is-ness*) precedes obligation (*ought-ness*). Before there are expectations, there is acceptance.

Knowing that God has chosen *us* reminds us that we are important to God. Knowing that God has bestowed spiritual blessings on us reminds that we have been forgiven and are no longer alienated from God.

Christians have been adopted into God's family. We are brothers and sisters in Christ, responsible for the care of others in Christ's community. Paul's opening words in the salutation reveal also our accountability to each other.

That God has lavished grace and conferred power on us gives us confidence that we can overcome adversity. All the forces this world can marshal against Christians pale in contrast to God's might. We have every resource we need to resist the evil in this world. We can be bold with the assurance of triumph as we have the hope, riches, and greatness of God's power. God's plan will not be thwarted.

The church completes the work of Christ. Christians are the visible body of Christ through which he continues to redeem and transform. The church models appropriate behavior as Christians are holy and faithful. As we live for God, the blessing comes full circle as our action brings further honor and praise to God.

TEACHING PLANS

Teaching Plan—Varied Learning Activities

Connect with Life

1. Ask the class whether anyone is or has been a member of an organization that restricted membership and that allowed members certain privileges or prestige. Examples could be athletic or extracurricular teams in school, professional or service organizations, honor societies, even commercial ventures such as frequent-flyer clubs. Lead a discussion with questions such as these, *What did you have to do to get in? What were some of the privileges or other advantages? What were some of the resources within the organization that were useful?*

State that we are about to begin our study of Paul's letter to the church in Ephesus. Refer to and summarize "Introducing Ephesians: Now, Through the Church," in the *Adult Bible Study Guide*. Emphasize that Ephesians is all about life in God's church, and this lesson is about the lavish blessings believers have as members of the church.

Guide Bible Study

2. Using the information in the small article in the *Study Guide* titled "Religious Life in Ephesus," and perhaps also other available resources, prepare a mini-lecture about Ephesus in the first century. Be sure to include information from Acts 19:23–31. Note that the city was located on an inland harbor with a short channel to the Aegean Sea. Since it was also at the crossroads of major trade routes, it was a prosperous, multicultural city, one of the most prominent in Asia Minor. Conclude the mini-lecture by asking the class to compare what they understand about Ephesus with their own community.

3. Read Ephesians 1:1–2. Then invite someone to read Ephesians 1:3–10 while the class listens for the word "blessed." Lead the class in brainstorming to generate a list of the *blessings God lavishes on us*. Write responses on the markerboard. Then, brainstorm to generate a second list—or highlight answers on the first list—of SPIRITUAL *blessings God lavishes on us*. Take a few moments to compare the two lists with the passage (Ephesians 1:1–10) and add any additional thoughts to the lists on the markerboard.

4. Enlist someone to read Ephesians 1:11–14. Ask, *What does this passage tell us about membership in God's church? What does it take to become a member?* Refer especially to verse 11 ("in Christ") and verse 13 ("believed in him").

   Note that some people fear that Christians can lose their salvation. Ask, *What do you think this passage tells us about the permanence of our salvation?* Refer especially to verses 13–14 ("marked with the seal of the promised Holy Spirit"; "the pledge of our inheritance toward redemption").

5. Have someone read Ephesians 1:15–23 while the class follows the reading and watches for what Paul prayed for the letter's readers. Prepare a worksheet with the following sentences and blanks. (A copy is available in "Teaching Resource Items" for this study at www.baptistwaypress.org.) You can provide one copy to each person or form small groups for a group exercise. (See Eph. 1:17–19a for words for the blanks.)

Read Ephesians 1:17–19a and complete this outline:

Paul prayed for God the Father to give believers a spirit of _____ and _____ so that they may _____.
Paul also prayed that _____
so that they may know _____,
_____, and _____.

Encourage Application

6. Divide the class into small groups of six or fewer people each. Provide paper and markers for each group. Say that your class has been asked to come up with marketing materials about membership in your church—advertisements, brochures, social media campaigns, etc. Instruct each group to take five minutes to prepare something that would promote your church to your community based on Ephesians 1. After a few minutes of work, call the group to attention again and ask each group to review their work to determine whether it conveys the spiritual blessings that are part of God's plan for the church as outlined in this passage of Ephesians. Then, allow another two to three minutes for revision. Call for each group to present their work.

7. Conclude with prayer as you (or another reader) re-read Ephesians 1:17–23. Consider using a different translation of the Bible from what you have used so far in this lesson.

Teaching Plan—Lecture and Questions

Connect with Life

1. Announce to the class that tomorrow will be *Super Power Day.* Each person will be given the super power of his or her choice for one twenty-four-hour period. Allow a minute or two for people to think about what one super power they would choose and what they would do with it. Call for responses, but monitor the time. After a time of sharing, say, *We are going to talk about the super power God has given to all believers and the other ways God has lavished spiritual resources on us.*

Guide Bible Study

2. Prepare and present a brief lecture about Ephesus (as described in Step 2 under "Teaching Plans—Varied Learning Activities").

3. Read, or have a volunteer read, Ephesians 1:1–10 as the class follows in their Bibles or the Scripture passage printed in their *Study Guides.* Instruct the class to look for words or phrases that describe ways God has lavished blessings on believers and perhaps to underline them. Invite responses.

   Refer to and read Ephesians 1:4 again. Offer insights on the meaning of the verse, using information in the *Study Guide* and in "Bible Comments" in this *Teaching Guide.*

4. Enlist someone to read Ephesians 1:11–14. Share information on these verses from the *Study Guide* and "Bible Comments" in this *Teaching Guide.* Call attention especially to the concept of a seal as a way to express ownership. Ask, *Can you think of some examples of seals or other ways that express a similar idea today?* Examples might include a sales receipt, writing a name on an item, a laundry mark, or wearing a T-shirt for a team or other organization. Then say, *Although the presence of the Holy Spirit is not visible, how does the Holy Spirit identify a believer as God's own possession, purchased by Christ's blood?*

5. State that Ephesians 1:3–10 outlines the blessings God has lavished on believers and verses 11–14 tell us about how we as believers have been chosen to be part of God's church. The next section, Ephesians 1:15–23, is Paul's prayer for believers to comprehend what these blessings of salvation promise. Have someone read Ephesians 1:15–23. Again, ask class members to watch for the words or phrases that indicate what Paul prays for believers, perhaps underlining them in their Bibles or *Study Guides*.

Refer to paragraph four of the section in the *Study Guide* under the heading, "We Are Known (1:15–23). Point out the sentences that read, "God has chosen the church for his own inheritance. We are valuable and precious to God." Then refer to the first sentence of the next paragraph, "Our experiences of church don't always match up with the spiritual reality." Ask the class to name some ways that the church, either your own church or the larger church, sometimes fails to match up with God's intentions. Ask, *Do you think that someone who is new to Christianity or to church-going would have different expectations of a church than someone who has been a church member for many years? In what ways? Why?*

After a few minutes of discussion, ask, *What might be some changes that would help ensure people's experiences match up with the spiritual ideal? in the church? in this class? in your personal actions and attitudes?*

Encourage Application

6. Recall the comments from step 1 regarding super powers that people would choose. Now say, *God has promised the super power of his Holy Spirit to dwell and work in us believers. Think about and envision the power of God's Spirit; then think of at least one thing that super power working in you could help you accomplish.* Allow a few moments for thought, and then invite people who are willing to do so to share their thoughts.

NOTES

1. Unless otherwise indicated, all Scripture quotations in lessons 1–4 and 8–11 are from the New Revised Standard Version.

FOCAL TEXT
Ephesians 2:1–10

BACKGROUND
Ephesians 2:1–10

MAIN IDEA
Only God's mercy, grace, and love, and not our goodness, make the difference in our experience of church and indeed of all of life.

QUESTION TO EXPLORE
What place does God's mercy, grace, and love have in your present experience of church and indeed of all of life?

TEACHING AIM
To lead adults to describe the difference God's mercy, grace, and love make for life now and forever

LESSON TWO

The Difference God's Love Makes

BIBLE COMMENTS

Understanding the Context

Ephesians 2:1–10 builds on the theme of salvation in Ephesians 1, which describes the spiritual blessings God bestowed on Ephesians and the enormous power given them in Christ. The first verses of chapter 2 might startle us. We might feel we have taken a step backwards. The uplifting words of chapter 1 have been replaced by a flashback to a harsh, stark description of humans' sinful plight. One effect of these verses, though, is to accent the love, mercy, and grace of God. One note that will help us understand this lesson's text is that every verb that addresses or refers to the readers is plural. Paul had the whole church in mind.

God has blessed Christians with every kind of spiritual blessing so that they lack nothing, and God has endowed them with the power to continue Christ's work on earth. Paul alluded to the bringing together of Jews and Gentiles into one body as he addressed both groups individually in the previous chapter (Ephesians 1:11–14). This lesson emphasizes God's saving work that brought the two groups together in Christ. Lesson three will focus on God's creation of one new group, Christians, out of previous enemies, Jews and Gentiles.

Paul taught in Ephesians, and in more detail in Romans 1—3, that all people are sinners. Ephesians 2:1–2 pictures Gentiles as dead in sins and controlled by the demonic prince of this world. Ephesians 2:3 expands the picture to Jews, who followed "the desires of flesh and senses." Without Christ, there is no hope.

God accomplished what was impossible for sinful humans to accomplish, raising them and giving them life. God blessed them with the power that had been bestowed on Christ. These blessings were only a foretaste of what God had planned for them.

Paul further developed his thoughts on salvation in verses 8–10. Without minimizing God's work, the role of the individual in receiving this salvation is clarified. The section ends with Paul teaching that works accompany salvation. A person's goodness cannot earn a person salvation, but doing good works is an essential part of one's saved life.

Interpreting the Scriptures

Dead in Sin (2:1–3)

2:1. Dividing verses 1–7 into two sections may be somewhat misleading, for they are one sentence in the Greek. The main verb of the sentence, "made us alive together," does not appear until verse 5.

Paul described the readers' condition as "dead through the trespasses and sins in which you once lived." The New Testament often uses the term *life* to describe a believer's union with Christ while describing nonbelievers with the word *death*. Being spiritually dead suggests alienation and separation from God and further notes the need for God's intervention to bring life. Only God can bestow spiritual life on those "dead" in sin. Placing "you" in an emphatic position in the Greek connects verse 1 with Ephesians 1:13–14, which was directed toward Gentile Christians.

Human sin causes spiritual death. Those who live apart from union with Christ are marked by sin. Paul underlined the devastating effects of sin by using two terms, "trespasses" and "sins." While their meanings overlap, "trespasses" suggests missing the mark or failures in the spiritual life. "Sins" denotes falling away from God's intentions or even neglect and inattention to spiritual matters.

2:2. Although the verb "made us alive" has yet to appear, Paul hinted at it when he used the past tense to describe their previous way of life. "Course of this world" distinguishes the life of people without God from those living in relationship with him. "World," which means either the universe or humanity living apart from Christ, contrasts the values and characteristics we regularly encounter with the heavenly or divine qualities Paul was touting. The expression may suggest the suffocating grip these values have on people.

Paul described this "world" as "following the ruler of the power of the air." This description derives from the ancient belief that demons lived in the atmosphere above the earth. We may no longer hold that ancient belief, but the reality of evil is obvious.

The "ruler" of this age is "the spirit" that leads people into disobedience. Paul was stressing the power of evil as it worked in the world. "Now at work" translates a Greek verb form that suggests a continuous action. The final phrase of the verse, "among those who are disobedient," makes clear that alienation from God is not an accidental or chance event, but a willful choice by people. Rebellion against God is universal.

2:3. The change of pronoun from "you" (2:1) to "us" and "we" shows that both Jews and Gentiles were alienated from God. "Them" refers back to the "disobedient" in the previous verse. Jews, like Gentiles, were controlled by the powers of this world, here described as "passions" and "desires" of the "flesh." "Flesh" is not one's physical body but the mind-set of self-centeredness. It depicts the person who is focused on self, not on God.

Those controlled by the sinful human nature stand under God's judgment ("were by nature children of wrath"). To stand against God is to bring judgment on oneself. The remaining verses in this lesson's Scripture text picture God's intervention that provides salvation.

Made Alive in Christ (2:4–7)

2:4. In this verse, the focus changes from the human condition to God's work to redeem people and unite them in Christ. God intervened in the lives of the spiritually dead because of compassion ("mercy") for those who could not make themselves alive. Paul was contrasting the wrath of God with the mercy of God. God loved humanity despite its sinfulness.

2:5–6. God revealed his mercy and love to the Ephesians both by giving them spiritual life and raising them from spiritual death. Paul might have been thinking of Christ's resurrection, their conversion experience, even their baptism. Determining the exact meaning does not appear necessary as all are interrelated. Christians were buried in Christ and united with his resurrection in their baptisms as they began their spiritual lives (see Romans 6:1–11).

God had delivered ("saved") the Ephesians. The verb form indicates that nothing could undo what God had done for them. God's work in raising them was linked closely to God's work in raising Jesus.

For comments on God's power and being seated "with him in the heavenly places in Christ Jesus," see "Bible Comments" in lesson one (especially on 1:20–21). In union with Christ, Christians find the power to live as believers in this world.

2:7. God's purpose in making people alive and seating them in places of God's power was to demonstrate divine grace. Christians have experienced only a part of God's grace, but what they have seen assures them that that grace will be sufficient for them in all circumstances. "Kindness" indicates God's love toward people through action.

Saved by Grace, for Good Works (2:8–10)

2:8–9. These words summarize much of what Paul had written in verses 1–7. Sinful humans have been saved and redeemed by God, not because of inherent goodness on their part, but because of God's undeserved favor toward them. The use of "grace" underscores God's willingness and desire to offer salvation. As in verse 5, the verb form of "have been saved" indicates a completed and permanent action.

"Faith" is an individual's response to God's grace. The word does not imply an intellectual assent but a turning to God because of a recognized need for God based on the realization of one's own inadequacies. One entrusts his or her life to the Lord completely.

One may wonder what Paul meant with the phrase, "it is the gift of God." Some have claimed that "it" refers back to "faith," but the word forms of both "it" and "faith" make this unlikely. "It" is a neuter pronoun while "faith" is feminine. More probably, "it" refers to the whole process by which a person is saved.

Paul further stressed that the process of salvation is God's work by adding the phrase, "not the result of works." "Boast" implies more than bragging. It signifies the confidence in one's personal ability to achieve salvation.

2:10. People are blessed by being saved. One purpose of a believer's salvation is to do good works. In using the word "created," Paul was highlighting God's initiative. Both God ("he") and "Christ" occupy a position of emphasis in this verse. God takes the initiative, one that ends in believers performing Christian deeds.

The phrase, "for good works," means more than that good works are the purpose of a new life. It actually denotes that good works are inseparable from one's salvation experience. To be a Christian is to be doing good works as a result of that new condition.

Focusing on the Meaning

God's love makes a difference. Sin has so marred the human condition that living apart from Christ is described as being spiritually dead. Paul went on to compare it to being enslaved to the spirit of disobedience that characterizes this world. To follow the values of this world is to reflect citizenship in an evil age. We live in a sinful state and are cut off from God.

God loved us when we were enslaved to the powers of this world. God sent Christ so that through him we might know God and God's salvation. Even a casual reading of these verses ought to convince us how much God loves us and how important we are to him.

Christians have experienced a radical change in nature. Through our faith in God's promises and our commitment to him, we have experienced resurrection in the present. We have been raised to places of power that guarantee our transformation into Christlikeness.

Being saved means performing good works. Paul has often been cast as stressing faith over against works. But *works* in such a discussion seems to be the keeping of law to attain righteousness. I believe that Paul would have affirmed that a person who has experienced salvation will inevitably do godly deeds in daily life. Salvation is more than having our ticket to heaven stamped.

Clearly, a person cannot earn salvation by his or her goodness or by doing good works. Only by the grace and mercy of God can human lives by transformed. However, let's not dismiss the importance of works, for Paul affirmed that we were "created in Christ Jesus for good works."

Good works are to characterize our new life in Christ, not just certain parts of it. Good works such as caring for the poor, seeking justice for the marginalized, and loving our neighbors are honorable. But doing good works also means that in our daily lives we demonstrate kindness, joy, acceptance, and love.

TEACHING PLANS

Teaching Plan—Varied Learning Activities

Connect with Life

1. Bring simple art supplies such as paper, scissors, tape or glue, colored markers or paints, and modeling clay. Provide enough for each person to have something to work with. As you distribute the materials, encourage everyone to create a "masterpiece." Allow about five minutes, and then have a brief show and tell.

   Alternatively, you could ask, *Does anyone have a hobby, craft, or other creative outlet? What is it?* Encourage everyone to think of something. Examples could be woodwork or needlework, music or art, but also computer programs, cooking, making friends, and so on. Then ask, *In this area of creativity, what would be a "masterpiece"?*

   Then state that people who live according to God's purpose are God's "masterpiece." In today's lesson we will affirm that only God's mercy, grace, and love—not our goodness or good works—are what make people God's masterpiece.

Guide Bible Study

2. Enlist someone to read Ephesians 2:1–3. Distribute paper and pen or pencil to each person. Ask each one to take a minute and write down a definition of *sin*. After a few minutes, call for responses. Without commending or disapproving, take note of the differences or similarities in the ways people define sin.

   Next, lead the class to brainstorm words, phrases, images that describe *spiritual death*.

   Ask, *Do you think more people are painfully aware of their sins and sinful nature, or do you think more people are in denial about their sins and sinful nature? Why?*

   During this discussion about sin, be sensitive to people who may be in the midst of a raw, emotional struggle with sin. Be prepared to take a moment of class time for prayer and/or to schedule a time this week for personal follow-up.

3. Read Ephesians 2:4–7. Say, *Think of a time that you were forgiven by someone or otherwise "let off the hook" for some offense or wrong you committed. How did that experience make you feel at the time? Did it have longer-lasting impact on you?*

    Say, *Because we have been forgiven and have received God's grace, we should in turn forgive and extend grace to others.* Ask the class as individuals to think of a person whom they need to forgive or to whom they have a chance to extend grace. Give several moments of private reflection. Challenge the class to pray about following through on this thought.

    Refer to question 4 near the end of the lesson in the *Study Guide*, "Even though we know we are saved by God's grace, why do we sometimes still act as if we have to earn God's favor?" Invite responses. Then ask, *In what ways do we sometimes still act as if we have to earn God's favor?*

4. Read Ephesians 2:8–10. Ask, *According to these verses, what do you think is God's purpose in saving us and turning us from our sins?*

    Ask, *What are some examples of how God displays his glory in nature?* Receive several answers, and then ask, *How does God display his glory through people? How can everyday Christians like you and me bring glory to God?*

Encourage Application

5. Say, *We have been concentrating in this lesson on ourselves as individuals with regard to receiving God's grace and mercy. What role does our church have in God's desire to extend grace and mercy to all who would receive it through faith?*

    Divide the class into small groups of six or fewer people each, and ask them to discuss the small article titled "Case Study" about Jamie in the *Study Guide*. If you like, reconvene after several minutes and ask for reports.

Teaching Plan—Lecture and Questions

Connect with Life

1. Ask, *Has anyone seen movies, TV shows, video games or books that depict a "dystopia," that is, a world after some kind of catastrophe?* (You may want to do an internet search for *dystopian movies* for examples.) Allow a few minutes for the class to talk about depictions of dystopias. Then ask, *Why are these depictions of dystopias disturbing? Do you think they might give a portrait of the world or one's life without the influence of God?*

    State that in today's lesson we will affirm that only God's mercy, grace, and love—not our goodness or good works—make the difference in our experience of church and all aspects of life.

Guide Bible Study

2. Read Ephesians 2:1–3. Lead the class to brainstorm a list of sins; write them on the markerboard. Examples might include stealing, murder, gossip, and so on. Ask, *Are some of these sins worse than others? If so, how would we rank them?* Allow the class to debate the issue.

    Lead a discussion with questions such as these: *Are you ever aware of your transgressions and sins? What makes you aware of them? Do you ever feel dead in your transgressions and sins?*

    Call attention to the third and fourth paragraphs of the lesson in the *Study Guide* under "Dead in Sin (2:1–3)." Point out that they include several ways people indulge in their cravings or desires. Ask, *Do you believe these are common? Are any of these familiar to you? What do these thoughts suggest about how easily and often we follow our own desires and cravings?* Then ask, *What are some strategies we can use to deal with the tension of our tendency to do our own thing versus living a holy life?*

3. Invite someone to read Ephesians 2:4–7. Ask, *What are some experiences you've had when you felt helpless and dependent on someone else for something? Can you think of a time when you wanted or needed something and got even more than you expected? What do these verses teach us about God?*

4. Enlist someone to read Ephesians 2:8–10. Call attention to Ephesians 2:8, and state that we are not saved because of our good works, but by God's grace, which we receive by faith. Ask, *What is the difference between doing good works in order to be saved versus doing good works as a result of thanksgiving that we have been saved?*

   Say, *Many people believe that doing good works or being a "good" person brings them favor in God's eyes and entry into heaven. How does this passage contradict that belief? How would you explain this to a non-believer?*

Encourage Application

5. Refer to and summarize "Implications and Actions" in the *Study Guide*. Focus on paragraph three, which begins, "Similarly, we should treat others. . . ." Ask, *In what ways do you think our church does this well? In what ways do you think we could improve?* Then ask, *Since each of us is part of the church, in what specific ways could we as individuals be part of our church's improvement?*

6. Distribute paper and pens to each person. Say, *Take a few moments and privately jot down any sins that are troubling you now. This will not be shared.* After a few minutes, say, *God hates these sins, big or small. But God loves you. This passage assures us that for those who are willing to believe God does so, God has mercy and grace to forgive our sins.* Pause for a few moments to let people ponder this. Then say, *If you are willing to accept God's mercy and grace by faith, tear up your paper and throw it away.* If you like, pass a wastebasket or other receptacle to gather the scraps of paper.

FOCAL TEXT
Ephesians 2:11–22

BACKGROUND
Ephesians 2:11–22

MAIN IDEA
God in Christ has made it possible for a church composed of people who formerly disagreed with, disliked, and even hated one another to be united through Christ's work on behalf of all of them.

QUESTION TO EXPLORE
If the unity of Christians is so important, why has the church as a whole never had it, why is it so hard to have even in a local church, and how can it be attained?

TEACHING AIM
To lead the group to describe the unity God has made possible in Christ and identify how we can move toward that unity today, beginning with their own church

LESSON THREE
The Church—Meant to Be United

BIBLE COMMENTS

Understanding the Context

One way of studying history is to focus on the wars that seem to be per-petually occurring.

Coveting of territory, vying for political and economic superiority, making attempts at gathering natural resources held by one group but wanted by another—these lie at the heart of such conflicts. In addition, theological differences sometimes are the root causes of wars.

The breadth and depth of violence of people on other people is appalling. If conflicts do not result in actual, literal violence, they can also manifest themselves in covert ways that can be almost as destruc-tive as actual physical violence.

The passage under examination highlights one of the primary realms of animosity in the first century A.D., that of the poor relations between Jews and Gentiles. *Gentiles* referred to everyone else in the Jewish world. Even the early church did not escape this conflict but had to deal with it (see the Book of Acts, especially Acts 10—11; 15).

The Apostle Paul knew of this conflict first hand and had been a part of the Jewish rejection of Gentile ways. With his conversion to Christianity, Paul experienced an approach to life that showed that even the ancient animosities between Jews and Gentiles had already been alleviated, at least in an ideal sense. Because of Christ, Paul realized that the possibility for warring parties to become at peace with one another was at hand.

Interpreting the Scriptures

Jews and Gentiles Apart, Now Together? (2:11–13)

2:11–12. "Remember," Paul said in verse 11. Memory, especially with regard to how God had walked with, moved ahead of, provided backup, and watched over the people of God in the Old Testament, was an important value, even virtue, to hold and keep active. The Gentiles in

Ephesus were not necessarily schooled in Hebrew history so as to under-stand the value of having such a memory about faith practice. Even so, Paul called them to "remember" the situation of their lives in the past. Gentiles could "remember" well enough to know what their situation had been.

Paul acquainted the Gentiles with how the circumstances were dire for anyone outside the covenant relationship with God. In this state, the Gentiles were people "having no hope and without God in the world," according to Paul.

Anyone without hope is one who has nothing for which to live. "Having no hope" toward anything bountiful in this life or the next communicates the state of utter despair in which Paul said people lived without Christ.

Paul provided a reality check for the Jews as well in these verses. Evidently, for many Jews "circumcision" had become considered to be something of a free ticket for people who were Jews in name only. These Jews were in no better position with God than the uncircumcised Gentiles.

2:13. Paul artfully pulled his audience out of the past into the present with "but now." Paul showed that life can be different. Circumstances and contexts that were dire can now be hopeful, because of the death of Christ but most importantly because of his resurrection. The good news of Jesus' life, ministry, crucifixion, and resurrection gave possibility for the Gentiles to be "brought near." In fact, because of Christ, anyone, no matter what race, nationality, or any other qualifier might be imposed, now can have access to God.

A Dividing Wall Taken Down (2:14–16)

2:14. Paul noted that the decline, even disappearance, of hostilities among Gentiles and Jews was already a reality because of Christ. First, Jesus being God in flesh became the basis for a reign of peace. Second, the wall in Jerusalem on which were statements excluding Gentiles from entrance into the temple was metaphorically broken down. Although the wall with its warning signs was still standing physically, it no longer represented a legitimate barrier to interchange with God. Any theologi-cal or philosophical wall intended to hold Jews superior to Gentiles was effectively broken down. In short, anything that fed hostility and conflict no longer had any substance.

2:15–16. Paul asserted that Jesus' work removed the law as the basis for relationship with God. As well, Jesus' life and death made way for the possibility of salvation for anyone. Any *ism*—such as racism, ageism, sexism—that pits portions of humanity against one another is nowhere near the will of God. Now, because of God's actions in Christ, the promise arises for "one new humanity."

Peaceful Saints (2:17–19)

2:17. Paul continued his analysis of Jesus' purpose for coming to humanity. Jesus articulated and demonstrated the essence and substance of the Hebrew understanding of *shalom*—"peace." *Shalom* in Jewish thought was an all-encompassing idea. In the Hebrew language, one can begin with any of the ethical words, righteousness for instance, and before long one would be in the middle of *shalom*. *Shalom*, "peace," was a greeting, a state of being, the substance of the hope that all creation was and would be under the care of God. *Shalom* could be considered a synonym for salvation. Jesus incarnated *shalom*. His miracles depicted the facets of *shalom*. The peace Christ provided extended to people who were "far off"—the Gentiles—as well as to people who were "near"—the Jews.

2:18. The dynamic portrayal of peace by Jesus' life and ministry had application for any person. "Both of us"—both Gentiles and Jews—now had "access in one Spirit to the Father." As Paul wrote in Galatians 3:28, "There is no longer Jew or Greek, there is no longer slave or free, there is no longer male and female; for all of you are one in Christ Jesus."

2:19. "So then" is another of Paul's characteristic transitional conjunctions. "So then"—as the result of Christ's work in being "our peace," any who are receptive to this peacemaking become part of the family of God. No reason is left for divisions among people, especially those who are part of the church. As described in verse 12, any touched by this peacemaking are now part of the family of God, no longer "aliens" or "strangers," but now full citizens in the kingdom of God.

Architectural Images (2:20–22)

2:20–21. The architectural metaphor Paul used in these verses likely will not be as familiar to readers now as it was to the Ephesian Christians. As they walked around the city, they observed Greco-Roman structures every day. They knew the importance of a foundation and a cornerstone. The buildings of the time in Ephesus were constructed almost completely of stone. The cornerstone was the first stone of the foundation laid. From its position, the rest of the foundation and the structure itself found reference. The cornerstone was of primary importance. Thus Paul referred to "Christ Jesus himself as the cornerstone." The foundation was secondary in importance, but important nonetheless.

"The foundation of the apostles and prophets" called readers to acknowledge the importance of previous servants of God. "Apostles" refers to those who had had direct acquaintance, conversation, and experience, with Jesus (see Acts 1:21–26). Paul's reference to "prophets" could have included both the foretelling and forth-telling definitions of being a prophet (see Acts 15:32; 21:10–11). The gift of such prophecy had already been displayed among the early Christians.

Paul amplified these architectural images with his thought that not only does the structure, the church, become joined together through Christ, but also there is a sense in which all of these are living stones. For, with the joining together, a development begins that eventuates into a "holy temple."

2:22. Once these Christians saw themselves in the manner in which Paul described, they would see that they were "built together spiritually into a dwelling place for God."

Focusing on the Meaning

This session explores Paul's observation that although the Ephesian church was made up of authentic Christians, they still held onto some of their reservations toward people not like themselves. The ideal, which they had not obtained, was that Christ's work had made available a unity among Christians unlike anything they had imagined. Their holding onto encultured ways of dealing with people different from them was counter to the gospel and counter-productive to expanding the delivery of the gospel.

We may, in the twenty-first century, begin to piously intone how off track those Ephesians became. That congregation was one of the seven churches reviewed in the Book of Revelation. Years after Paul's correspondence with them they were praised for their patient endurance and intolerance for evildoers, but they were indicted and reprimanded for abandoning the love they had at first (Revelation 2:4). The phrase "the love" can be interpreted as encompassing the Ephesians' understanding at one point in their congregation's existence of the ideal Paul put in front of them. They realized they were one in Christ. They lived life in a loving communion that bridged any dynamics that would pull their attention away from God in Christ. They allowed the Spirit to guide their actions within and without their congregation. Any relationships they had were filtered through their relationship with Christ. Revelation 2:4 suggests they had moved away from this ideal.

As we are honest with ourselves, any of us can look no further than our own congregation to realize how far we are from the unity for which Paul called. Moreover, we most likely resemble more the era of the Ephesian church that left the love it had at first. How much better would our witness about and with Christ be if we abandoned all those means and schemes that continually divide us rather than abandoning what we loved first—Christ's message and acts as described in these verses in Ephesians? How much more would we understand the sense of living life with a higher quality if we were more unified in relationships than divided?

TEACHING PLANS

Teaching Plan—Varied Learning Activities

Connect with Life

1. Ask, *Has anyone ever tried to make salad dressing with just oil and vinegar? What happens when you try to mix them?* Stress that they are difficult to mix; they separate quickly, even after stirring or shaking. Then ask, *What happens if you add some egg yolk to the oil and vinegar and then mix vigorously? That's how you make mayonnaise, and it is a whole new substance that will stay mixed for a long time.* If you like, bring a small amount of vinegar and salad oil, plus an egg and a jar of mayonnaise and display each of these as you talk. (If this approach doesn't fit your class, refer to and summarize the opening illustration in the lesson in the *Study Guide.*)

    Say, *This is an illustration of what we will discuss today: the unity that God has made possible in Christ. We will also learn to identify how we can move toward that unity—beginning with our church.*

Guide Bible Study

2. Enlist someone to read Ephesians 2:11–13. State that the *Study Guide* points out that "Jews celebrated the law for helping them maintain purity and keeping them separate from the nations around them." Ask, *In what ways was this separation good for the Jewish people? In what ways was this separation not good for the Jewish people? How did they view people who were not Jews?* Refer to Ephesians 2:12, and ask, *Do you think that "outsiders" to the Christian faith realize what they are missing as members of the body of Christ? What approach would you take to explain it to a non-believer?*

3. Invite someone to read Ephesians 2:14–18. Lead the class to identify the contrast in these verses to verses 11–13 based on what Christ has done.

Help the class to count how many churches there are within a short distance from your own church. Note how many of them are Baptist. Then ask, *Why do you think there are so many churches? Why do you think there are so many Baptist churches in such a small area?*

Refer to verse 15, and ask, *Do you think that God's ultimate goal is making peace among people or between people and God? How does one relate to the other? What is our part in each of these?*

4. Have someone read Ephesians 2:19–22. Use information on these verses in the *Study Guide* and in "Bible Comments" in this *Teaching Guide* to clarify their meaning. Then lead a discussion with questions such as these: *Can you think of some places or events where a wide variety of people come together in unity and harmony?* (An example might be a parade for a winning sports team.) *Have you ever participated in one of these? How would you describe the feelings or the actions of yourself or others who were involved? To what do you attribute the feelings of unity and harmony?* Refer to and call for responses to question 3 near the end of the lesson in the *Study Guide.*

Encourage Application

5. Refer to "Implications and Actions" in the lesson in the *Study Guide,* and point out the various ways in which churches can divide—age groups, economic strata, race, gender, families, factions, cliques, longevity in the church. Write these differences on the markerboard and ask the class to add any others they can think of. Then, for each, draw a line, labeling one end "Very" and the other "Not at all." Ask the class how they would rate your church as being divided by these different factors. For example, if your church kept men and women on separate floors of the church, you might rank it "Very" divided for gender. Work through the different factors, and conclude with an evaluation of your church. Then lead a discussion with questions such as these: *Do you think our church would be stronger and more in line with God's purpose if some of these divisions were less pronounced? What are some things that our church could do to lessen the differences? What are some things this class could do as a group?*

What are some things that we could do as individuals? How does this passage inspire us to work through any divisiveness in our church?

6. As an alternative or in addition, divide the class into small groups and ask each group to discuss the small article titled "Case Study" in the *Study Guide*. After about five minutes of discussion, reconvene the groups and call for brief reports.

Teaching Plan—Lecture and Questions

Connect with Life

1. Write the word "Alien" on the markerboard. Ask the class to brainstorm as many meanings or images as they can come up with. You can add to the discussion with a dictionary definition if you like. After a few minutes, ask, *Have you ever felt like an alien? Can you think of someone who was "alien" to you whom you met at church?* Take a few personal responses.

   Be aware that different translations of the text use other terms for "aliens." Some use "foreigners" or "strangers," and you can include or substitute those terms for "alien" if you like.

   Then say, *People can be alienated from one another, and people can be alienated from God. Today we will learn that God in Christ has made it possible for a church composed of diverse or "alien" people to be united through Christ's work on behalf of all of them.*

Guide Bible Study

2. Read Ephesians 2:11–13. State that the *Study Guide* compares the relationship between Jews and Gentiles during the first century with the relationship between races in the United States. Invite the class to compare and contrast these two sets of relationships.

   Ask volunteers to look up and read some other Scripture verses related to circumcision, as follows: Deuteronomy 10:16; 30:6; Romans 2:29; Colossians 2:11–12.

3. Read Ephesians 2:14–18. Explain these verses using information on them in the *Study Guide* and in "Bible Comments" in this *Teaching Guide*. Ask, *In verse 16, does the term "hostility" refer to hostility between people and God or between the different groups of people (for example, Jews and Gentiles)? When you think about the congregation in this church, what are some of the differences among people? For example, there are differences in age and gender; what else?* If you like, make a list of differences on the markerboard. Ask, *Compared to other churches, do you think our church people are more alike or less alike one another?*

Continue the discussion with questions such as these: *How united do you think we as a church are? Do you think there are barriers to or levels of participation in our church? in the whole Christian church? What do you think some of these barriers or levels might be? What do you think it would take to eliminate or minimize these barriers or levels?*

4. Read Ephesians 2:19–22 Ask for volunteers to look up and read from their Bibles some or all of the following verses: Genesis 12:2–3; Psalm 67:1–2; Isaiah 42:6, 49:6; Matthew 28:19–20; Luke 2:28–32; 24:46–47; Acts 1:8; 13:47. Ask, *What do you think these verses tell us about God's plan for reaching out to all the peoples of the world?*

Note that in Ephesians 2:22, Paul says that we become a dwelling in which God lives by his Spirit. Lead a discussion with questions such as these: *How do you feel about being a dwelling place for God? Does it imply any responsibilities? Does it require any changes in the ways you think, speak, or act?*

Encourage Application

5. Refer to and lead the class to respond to the questions near the end of the lesson in the *Study Guide*. As time permits, also read and consider the "Case Study" in the *Study Guide*.

FOCAL TEXT
Ephesians 3

BACKGROUND
Ephesians 3

MAIN IDEA
In light of the mission God has given the church, the church needs God's strength and for Christ and his love to dwell in the hearts of its members.

QUESTION TO EXPLORE
What should be included in a prayer for your church?

TEACHING AIM
To lead adults to evaluate the extent to which they recognize the mission to which God has set the church and to identify ways for receiving spiritual strength for fulfilling it

LESSON FOUR
The Church's Mission, the Church's Needs

BIBLE COMMENTS

Understanding the Context

If one reads the New Testament with the idea of paradox in mind, rich insights will arise from the passages. The essence of paradox is that two or more apparently incongruent ideas, themes, or topics fit together when one steps back to see the larger picture.

Ephesians 3 presents a whole package of paradoxes. In this chapter, the reader can begin to explore Paul's tendency toward using the pattern of paradox throughout his writings.

In the case of this portion of the letter to the Christians at Ephesus, Paul used paradox with regard to the inclusion of Gentiles in the faith stream of relationship to God. They had been *outside,* and now they were *inside* (see Ephesians 3:6). Paul had been a leader in Judaism, and now he projected himself as a servant of God, the least of all the saints (see Eph. 3:7–8). A mystery had abounded since the dawn of humanity, but now Paul could provide the answer to the riddle (see 3:9). The church has inherited the delegation of God's message of grace, but the church itself is in great need of grace (see 3:16).

Another paradox in the passage is that although the gospel provided the basis for a life well lived, suffering still was a part of life for even God's children. Understanding a life of suffering, Paul encouraged the Ephesians not to lose heart, faint, or become so discouraged for living through whatever suffering Paul or they themselves experienced (see 3:13).

As you and your class study Ephesians 3, allow the passage to expand your perspective about the paradoxes from God. Doing so can result in renewed worship of God.

Interpreting the Scriptures

Paul Among the Gentiles (3:1–6)

3:1–2. "This is the reason" is a concise summary of Ephesians 1—2. Paul's calling from God was to take the gospel to the Gentiles. In Paul's charge lay the need to proclaim the ramifications and imperatives of that calling. The Ephesians needed to understand that through Christ all the cultural barriers to good relationships between people, with special reference to Jews and Gentiles, had come down. And, anyone confessing Christ should begin living in light of such realities.

3:3–4. The emphasis in Ephesians 1—2 concerning the unity of all people went against the grain of the cultural and theological assumptions of the time. The Jews considered themselves special. The Hellenistic world was a class society with Roman citizens at the top. The idea of unity among people was a puzzle, a mystery, a paradox. The keys to that mystery had been "made known" to Paul "by revelation."

3:5–6. Indeed, "this mystery" had now been "made known to humankind, as it has now been revealed to his holy apostles and prophets by the Spirit." See the comments on Ephesians 2:20–21 in lesson three concerning "apostles and prophets." Note also how Ephesians 3:6 summarizes and expands the thought of Ephesians 2:11–22. The Gentiles now "have become fellow heirs, members of the same body, and sharers in the promise in Christ Jesus through the gospel."

The Mystery of the Ages (3:7–12)

Paul provided historical context so the Ephesians could demystify the mystery and also become interpreters and deliverers of the mystery. Paul's implicit question hangs in the air for us, too: *Does your understanding of the gospel hold to this basic truth: the good news is for any and all of God's human creations, not just a privileged few?*

3:7–8. Paul recognized that a true follower of Christ should become the servant of others. Such a characterization required the transformation of one's ego. The servant image was even too high a category for Paul as he identified himself as "the very least" (3:8) of all the possibilities for being the proclaimer of "this mystery" (3:5).

3:9. Paul perceived his role of being God's "servant" as a "gift of God's grace" (3:7), the same grace that he proclaimed to the Ephesians. This grace gave Paul the courage to take his message to anyone. Paul's God-given work was "to make everyone see what is the plan of the mystery hidden for ages in God who created all things." The church of Ephesus—and all the readers of the letter—needed to assume the same charge.

3:10. The message of the grace of God to all people, part of the mystery, was to be delivered by the church to itself and to the culture. The church would provide witness even to the "the rulers and authorities in the heavenly places." Even the angelic hosts did not understand the full measure of God's plan for creation. Thus the church formed a major part of the mechanism for God's work of redemption on earth and beyond.

3:11–12. The Ephesians had only to align themselves with this masterful plan. This was the path to living out the mystery. Appearing here is one of the most concise statements in the New Testament of the what, why, and how of living the Christian life through the church. Paul highlighted an idea we may neglect. Christians are to live boldly and confidently—with courage.

Paul's Concern for the Gentiles (3:13–21)

These verses form an extraordinarily profound section of the whole letter. As Paul had meticulously explored deep theology, his reflective journey pushed him into a worship mode.

3:13. The paragraph break should come with this verse. Paul's prayer arose from his theological reflections. Notice that Paul prayed "for" the Ephesians, not at them or self-centeredly for himself. The prayer begins with further encouragement, that the Ephesians would not "lose heart"—lose courage, hope, confidence—so as to become indifferent to the gospel and remove themselves from its influence.

A subtle reference to "my sufferings" indicates the level of relation-ship between Paul and the Ephesian Christians. Their sense of going into the future with the gospel hinged on Paul's leadership. His absence and his difficulties could provide reason for them to despair, but Paul prayed they would not let that happen.

3:14–15. "For this reason" is Paul's repeated use of the transitional, conjunctive phrase in 3:1 where Paul's overall thought began. The Greek words are the same in both cases. Ephesians 3:1 really is the beginning of the prayer that gathers momentum in 3:13 and continues beginning in 3:14. The content between verses 1 and 14 is not to be considered mere digression. Rather, Paul knew he needed to place his prayer in the context of the larger narrative of redemption history.

Paul referred to one of the postures for prayer for then and now—"I bow my knees." This body language of utter humility before God reflects the inner consciousness before God.

Note the Trinitarian perspective that moves through Paul's prayer. With verses 14–15, "Father" is intoned. In verses 16–17 appear "Spirit" and "Christ." Although the Trinity is not put forward in the New Testament as a doctrinal construct, here the mention of "Father," "Christ," and "Spirit" points to such a concept.

3:16–17. Paul emphasized the place of the "inner being." The "inner being" is that part of humans out of which comes actions that can be marked by the integrity of the character of God. Paul prayed for the Spirit's power and for Christ to dwell in his readers' hearts.

3:18–19. Paul prayed that these Christians to whom he wrote might "comprehend," not just identify and describe, the mystery of the gospel. He wanted them to understand it so well as to live it. Paul's prayer was that the comprehension would move among all the saints, all believers. And Paul prayed that the letter's readers would "know the love of Christ that surpasses knowledge"—any knowledge. The result would be that they would "be filled with all the fullness of God," another concept that stretches the imagination.

3:20–21. Paul closed his prayer with words intended to draw us to awe and wonder. Moreover, such a prayer encourages us to live such a life. To have God's power "within us" means not just alongside us, but truly living within us in an intimate way, nourishing our spirits, informing and forming our minds, and providing what we need to live the Christian life.

Focusing on the Meaning

The priesthood of the believer has been and continues to be an important concept for Baptists. The significance of every individual making her or his own decisions about the will of God, interpreting Scripture according to her or his own God-led conscience, cannot be over-estimated. The idea finds resonance throughout the New Testament. The Reformers re-discovered the principle. In twenty-first century American culture, however, the concept has been absorbed into the overt individualism that is rampant in our society. The egocentric, what's-in-it-for-me-right-now impulse characterizes our way of life, and it also subverts the priesthood concept.

The priesthood of the believer concept works best for the sake of the gospel and the church when we recognize we are to live out our faith in relation with other believers. We need each other in living life and in being Christian. We are created not merely to seek our own interests but also to live in relationship with others. Truly absorbing the gospel and living in Christ through the power of the Spirit helps us understand that we are part of the people of God and not just individual believers. We will be better for ourselves and others as we recognize we are in the stream of those who have followed God's plan for the ages, are moving in that stream now, and have something to do with shaping the course of the stream in the future. These ideas are paradoxical, but in the course of losing ourselves we find our real selves.

TEACHING PLANS

Teaching Plan—Varied Learning Activities

Connect with Life

1. Bring a bag of candy or some other desirable treat. Show it to the class and announce that you feel as if it should be shared with others, but it's extremely valuable. Ask the class for recommendations on whom to share it with and those with whom you should not share it. Encourage the class to think big and be playful in this discussion. After a few minutes, ask, *What about the gospel of God's grace, love, and forgiveness? Are there some people with whom we should share or not share?* Again, allow a bit of discussion.

    Say, *Today we will explore the church's mission to proclaim the gospel and how it should prompt us to pray that God will grant us the strength, love, and power to fulfill it.*

Guide Bible Study

2. Ask the class to listen for what Ephesians 3:1–13 says about how Paul saw his mission. Read Ephesians 3:1–13. Ask the class whether they know what your church's mission or mission statement is. You may be able to find the mission statement in the church literature or on the website. If not, consider inviting someone from the church leadership to visit your class and explain the mission statement. Or, you can lead the class in a discussion to write a mission statement.

    Explain Ephesians 3:1–13 using information on these verses in the *Study Guide* and in "Bible Comments" in this *Teaching Guide*.

3. Enlist someone to read Ephesians 3:14–22 while the class listens for what Paul prayed for his readers.

    Refer to Ephesians 3:14. Distribute paper and pen to each person. Ask the class to write their names on the paper. Then say, *Everyone's name has a bit of a story. It may tell about their ancestry or it may tell something about their parents.* Ask them to write down what they would like their names to tell someone about themselves. After a few minutes, invite members to make comments. Then say, *If we truly lived as if our names came from God, how do you think we would live? How might we change our name to reflect that "every family in heaven and on earth" derives its name from the Father?*

4. Note that Paul's prayer is that we would have the *strength, love* and *power* to live for God and proclaim the gospel. Divide into three groups. Assign one of these terms—*strength, love,* and *power*—to each group and instruct them to answer the question, *Why do we as believers need this for proclaiming the gospel effectively?* After about three to five minutes of discussion, call for reports.

   Explain Ephesians 3:14–22 further by using information on these verses in the *Study Guide* and in "Bible Comments" in this *Teaching Guide.*

Encourage Application

5. Ask, *Has anyone ever been part of a group or team that was involved in an effort to proclaim the gospel or accomplish a mission on behalf of Christ? What effect did being part of a team—as opposed to operating solo—have?*

   Continue the discussion by asking, *Why does our mission to glorify God by proclaiming and living the gospel require spiritual strength that only God can supply? What are some ways that people can receive spiritual strength for fulfilling God's mission?*

6. Conclude by distributing the candy or other treat referred to in step 1. Encourage everyone in the class to be bold and generous in sharing the gospel of God's grace, love, and forgiveness.

Teaching Plan—Lecture and Questions

Connect with Life

1. Ask the class whether they know of any dramatic stories of people whose lives have been transformed by the gospel. Point to the first

paragraph of the lesson in the *Study Guide*. After some response, stress that these dramatic conversions are evidence of the power of the gospel to transform anyone. Then ask the class to tell of less dramatic examples (their own, perhaps). Ask, *What do these stories of conversion tell us about what kinds of people can be transformed by the gospel? Are there any people who are beyond the reach or influence of the gospel?*

Say, *In this lesson, as we study Ephesians we will seek to evaluate the extent to which we recognize the mission God has set before our church and identify ways for receiving spiritual strength for fulfilling it.*

Guide Bible Study

2. Read Ephesians 3:1–13 as the class listens for Paul's mission. Call attention to the term "mystery" in verse 5. Lead the class in a discussion with questions such as these: *What is the mystery to which Paul referred?* (Hint: see 3:6.) *How did Paul come to his understanding of the mystery? Is Paul the only person entrusted with this mystery? What is the responsibility for those who are entrusted with this mystery?*

Enlist someone to read verse 12. Invite the class to imagine themselves approaching God. Allow a moment for them to come up with a mental image. Now ask, *Do you see yourself approaching God with "boldness and confidence"? Why or why not? Ask, What does this passage teach us about the confidence to approach and interact with God?*

Read verse 13. Point out that Paul urged the readers not be to discouraged because of his sufferings for them. Guide discussion by asking questions like these: *Why do you think Paul's readers might have become discouraged about Paul's sufferings on behalf of Christ? Do we get discouraged by others' suffering on behalf of Christ? Do we get discouraged because of our own sufferings on behalf of Christ? Can suffering on behalf of Christ be motivational? Can it be de-motivating? Why and how?*

Point out that the *Study Guide* states under the subhead, "Stewards of Grace (3:1–13)," that "Paul did not regard his mission as a burdensome responsibility but a God-given opportunity." Ask, *When you think of sharing the gospel in your life circumstance, do you feel it is a burdensome responsibility or a God-given opportunity? or neither? or both? How can we counter the feeling that it is a burden?*

3. Enlist someone to read Ephesians 3:14–21, and ask the class to listen for the things Paul prayed for his readers. Note in 3:14 that Paul said, "I kneel before the Father" (NIV84). Lead a discussion with questions such as these: *What does kneeling signify? When do people kneel? Do people in our church kneel during worship? What are some other postures that communicate our feelings about someone or something? Besides kneeling, what are some other ways to show respect and submission to God? What are some things people say, think, or do that show disrespect toward God?*

   Call attention to verse 16. Use questions such as these to lead a discussion of this verse: *Do you ever feel as if your physical, emotional or spiritual resources are exhausted? When are some times that you have felt that way? What circumstances bring us to feeling exhausted? What are some ways we can refresh ourselves? What does this verse tell us about our access to God's spiritual resources?*

   Note that Ephesians 3:14–21 is a beautiful prayer that many people have learned by heart. Ask whether anyone has already memorized this passage. If so, ask what prompted them to learn it. Then, challenge the class to memorize the passage.

Encourage Application

4. Call attention to the small article titled, "Ways to Pray for Your Church," in the *Study Guide*. Lead the class in praying through each of these. You or a volunteer can read each listing and allow a moment of silence after each. You could also divide into small groups and assign one or more of these prayers to each group. Challenge each person to choose one item or more in the list to continue praying through the coming weeks.

FOCAL TEXT
Ephesians 4:1–16

BACKGROUND
Ephesians 4:1–16

MAIN IDEA
The church is to live in a manner worthy of its calling as the body of Christ.

QUESTION TO EXPLORE
What qualities of Christ does your church demonstrate?

TEACHING AIM
To lead adults to identify qualities and actions the church is to demonstrate as Christ's body

LESSON FIVE

The Church Fulfilling Its Calling

BIBLE COMMENTS

Understanding the Context

Having studied the first three chapters of Ephesians, class members will not be surprised to sense a change in direction at the beginning of this fourth chapter of Paul's letter. Thus far, Paul has provided a rather sweeping presentation of the magnificent work of God through Christ. The great missionary celebrated the abundant grace of God as manifested in the offer of salvation through Christ. He has focused on the overwhelming love of God as the catalyst for a different way of life for those who comprise the church. In light of this grace and love, God provides the church the strength and the unity that the family of faith needs to be who God has designed the church to be.[1]

In the fourth chapter, the tenor of the letter shifts to a call for the church to respond to what God has done through Christ. As is typical of Pauline writings, it is not enough to discuss, or even to celebrate, the powerful work of God through Christ. The church is not being the church until the people respond to what the work of God calls them to do. As a metaphor of worship in many churches, the Ephesian letter shifts from the opening hymn of praise to the final hymn of commitment.

This new direction toward a call to respond to what God has done is emphatically noted at the beginning of Ephesians 4. Paul's inclusion of the transitional word "then" (Ephesians 4:1) clearly warned the readers that what followed ought to be a result of what had already been written. Because God "has blessed us in the heavenly realms with every spiritual blessing in Christ" (Eph. 1:3), "then" (4:1) we must respond as the church ever faithful.

Interpreting the Scriptures

The Unity of the Calling (4:1–6)

4:1. The movement of Paul's thought from the doctrinal (chapters 1—3) to the practical (chapters 4—6) is dramatic. Not only is there the transitional word "then," but there is also the admonition "to live a life worthy of the calling." Paul had already noted that the church's calling as the body of Christ involves God's love, mercy, grace, unity, and mission. Now, it was time to turn the task over to the church to put into reality the life that God has called the church to live. The text of this lesson introduces the practical application of the truths contained in Ephesians 1—3.

4:2. The journey to being "worthy" of God's calling initially involves four characteristics. Christians ought to be "humble," a quality that inherently prevents Christians from allowing this calling to become a matter of ego. The next attribute is *gentleness,* which calls Christians to trust that what comes from God is good and should not be resisted. Paul further urged his readers to "be patient," perhaps in reference to long-suffering in light of being wronged. The last distinction is "bearing with one another in love." This fourth quality suggests that Christians sometimes have to endure the wrong behavior of fellow Christians in love.

4:3–6. The focus turns toward a primary theme throughout Ephesians: the unity of the church. Paul had already addressed this concept, most specifically in Ephesians 2:1–22 and 3:14–21. For a study of this theme of unity, see lesson three. In this passage, the goal of unity is to place it squarely in the context of the church's work to become worthy of its calling as the body of Christ.

Unity is built on the active evidence of the four qualities mentioned in verse 2. There is a logical reason to live with humbleness, gentleness, patience, and endurance toward each other, because all Christians share "one body," "one Spirit," "one hope," "one Lord, one faith, one baptism," and "one God." The commonality of Christians far outweighs their differences.

The Grace of the Calling (4:7–13)

As suggested in the *Study Guide* in "Studying *Letters to the Ephesians and Timothy: Guidance for the Church and Its Leaders,*" the Letter to the Ephesians may actually have been a letter intended for a large number of churches, instead of one specific church in Ephesus. This use of the writing as a circular letter is further supported by the way the readers are often addressed in plural form. A common concern among all of these first-century churches must have been how they were going to live out their calling as the one body of Christ. Since they came from both Jewish and Gentile backgrounds, their work toward unity would be difficult at best.

4:7. Being called to unity amidst this diversity is a positive result of Christ's grace. Christ "apportioned" this grace to every believer. As only Christ could wisely determine, each Christian receives gifts to contribute individually to the kingdom. Importantly, the varied gifts ought not to erode the unity of the body.

4:8–10. To illustrate the giving of gifts from the abundance of Christ, Paul alluded to the psalmist's description of God as the victorious King (Psalm 68:18). The conquering king would ascend to his throne, receiving the gifts of triumph, ultimately delivering those gifts to his people (Ps. 68:9–10). The metaphor is that Christ has ascended to his throne as well, following his descent to earth to live among the creation. In Christ's victory at the cross, he took captive such enemies as sin, the evils of this world, and ultimately, death itself.

4:11–13. Christ gives his followers gracious gifts, including different assignments to carry out their unique callings. He distributes them as he knows best. The gifts enable his followers to be worthy of their calling as the body of Christ. Some are called to be "apostles," a unique designation for a messenger who is sent out to tell others about Christ. In the context of Ephesians, an "apostle" is one who is commissioned to tell the story of Christ to the Jewish and Gentile world. Some are called to be "prophets" to serve as God's spokespeople, interpreting a specific message from God. "Evangelists" have a similar assignment, distinguishable as heralds who deliver the good news of Jesus. "Pastors" are called to care for God's people, as shepherds care for their flock. Finally, "teachers" fulfill the task of explaining the teachings about Jesus.

Essential to this list of assignments is a singular purpose for all of them. God calls each of them "to prepare God's people for works of service, so that the body of Christ may be built up." Whatever the specific calling, both clergy and laity ultimately have the responsibility to build up the body of Christ. Not only does this common intent keep those who are called focused on their respective missions, but it also removes any sense that one Christian has higher value over another. All Christians have the same goal of working in unity to edify the body of Christ.

The Unity of Grace (4:14–16)

4:14. Reading Paul's letter demands that we interpret the conditions of its recipients. Based on Paul's hope that "we will no longer be infants," his current assessment was that those who received the Ephesians letter were subject to the influence of the next deceptive wind or crafty wave. He perceived that these Christians were not steadfast in their calling.

4:15–16. Ultimately, the goal was that these infants would "grow up into him who is the Head, that is, Christ." As Christians become more like Christ, they fulfill their calling more completely as the people of God. Summarily, the grace of God is given to each believer, so that the unity of his or her service will bring about the realization of the calling as the body of Christ.

Focusing on the Meaning

Christians should constantly discover what qualities and actions demonstrate and fulfill the calling as the body of Christ. The tendency may be to place the burden on the church as a whole, even on the local church where believers attend. Whenever the charge falls on the total group, individual members of the body can be tempted to divest personal accountability and responsibility—instead leaving it to the person in the other pew. Each Christian ought to consider his or her personal calling for the unity of the body.

On the other end of the spectrum, those of the Baptist tradition may encourage individuality to the detriment of the shared life that this passage promotes. Sometimes our failure to see the whole picture of the Baptist emphasis on each person's distinct responsibility as a priest before God may cause the impact of these words to go unrealized to their fullest extent. Taken to the level of churches' working together as the body of Christ, Baptist autonomy may further be problematic in an effort to promote unity in the body of Christ. Given that these Baptist distinctives are an important part of our heritage, how might Baptists and their churches fulfill the calling of this Ephesians letter?

A larger threat across the whole of Christianity is the consumer-oriented lifestyle of so many people within churches today. As believers select churches and church activities as though they are choosing from a restaurant menu, this passage forces a startling contrast. Instead of deciding which church best fits one's personal needs and wants, the Letter to the Ephesians calls Christians to select their involvement based on calling, all working in unity toward the building up of the body. To be worthy of the calling is to be united in the calling, selflessly working toward the Christlikeness of the church.

TEACHING PLANS

Teaching Plan—Varied Learning Activities

Connect with Life

1. Prior to the class session, place a copy of the lesson handout, "Top 10 Things That Annoy Me about the Church" in the seat of each learner. (A copy of the lesson handout is available in "Teaching Resource Items" for this study at www.baptistwaypress.org.)

Top 10 Things That Annoy Me About the Church

10. _____

 9. _____

 8. _____

 7. _____

 6. _____

 5. _____

 4. _____

 3. _____

 2. _____

 1. _____

---

2. Begin the class with a partnering-in-prayer exercise. Direct learners to listen to your instructions before they take any action. Instruct learners to:

   a. Sit next to another learner

   b. Share a specific request for prayer

   c. Allow the partner to pray for him or her and then in turn pray for the specific request of the partner

   d. Take about five minutes total for this time of prayer

   e. Stop praying when they hear you start praying

   f. Begin praying

3. At the five-minute mark, pray for God's blessing for this lesson.

4. Direct learners to gather in groups of three or four participants. Instruct them to use the lesson handout to develop a group list of things that annoy them about the church. They may wish to develop their individual lists first and then develop a group list. Allow about five-to-seven minutes for this exercise. (Completing all ten items is not a requirement.) Inform learners that they will need to select a spokesperson who will share with the class their "Top 10" list. Observe the class carefully. If groups have completed their assignment before the allotted time, move on to the next phase of the lesson. Give periodic updates as to the time remaining for the exercise.

5. Instruct the class to remain in their groups. Direct each group spokesperson to simply read their list and refrain from giving commentary. Encourage them to give brief clarification only where needed.

6. Lead learners in a brief class discussion. Ask learners: *Why do you think these things happen?*

7. Inform learners that this lesson is intended to help us identify qualities and actions the church should demonstrate as Christ's body.

Guide Bible Study

8. Refer to the *Study Guide* and the "Bible Comments" section in this *Teaching Guide* for assistance in understanding, explaining, and clarifying biblical material throughout the lesson.

9. Invite a volunteer to read Ephesians 4:1–6. Summarize and explain these verses. Direct learners to reorganize in their groups. Instruct them to discuss Paul's use of the following words and phrases. Ask: *What are the meanings of these words and phrases, and why did Paul use them?*
   a. "live a life worthy" (4:1)
   b. "be completely humble" (4:2)
   c. "be . . . gentle" (4:2)
   d. "be patient" (4:2)
   e. "bearing with one another in love" (4:2)
   f. "keep the unity" (4:3)

   (A copy of the questions for the group activity in steps 9, 10, and 11 is available in "Teaching Resource Items" for this study at www.baptistwaypress.org.)

10. Have a volunteer read Ephesians 4:7–13. Summarize and explain these verses. Direct learners to reorganize in their groups. Instruct them to discuss verses 11–13. Ask these questions: *What are the gifts given to the church? How do they operate? What is their purpose?*

11. Enlist a volunteer to read Ephesians 4:14–16. Direct learners to reorganize in their groups. Instruct them to identify the characteristics of the immature and the mature believer. Ask: *How is the immature*

believer described? How is the mature believer described? How does
each respond to the outer world?

Encourage Application

12. Summarize the lesson using information in "Meaning for Today" in the *Study Guide*. Make sure learners stay assembled in their groups.

13. Direct learners' attention back to their group "Top 10" list. Instruct them to review their list. Instruct them to apply principles of the passage to each issue on their list. They can simply write the verse or verses next to the issue to indicate the source of the appropriate teaching.

14. Direct learners in their groups to pray over their lists with the biblical correctives written on them. Conclude the class session with prayer.

Teaching Plan—Lecture and Questions

Connect with Life

1. Prior to class beginning, place a copy of the lesson handout of the partially completed outline of the lesson at each learner's place. Learners will fill in the blanks on the lesson handout as you teach. The lesson handout as well as a completed lesson outline (to be used by you to guide learners through the lesson) is available in "Teaching Resource Items" for this study at www.baptistwaypress.org.

2. Begin class with prayer.

3. Use the illustration "Lists" to begin the lesson.

Lists

Twenty-eight-year-old Wendy was a first-year third-grade teacher. Because of her busy life routine she found it hard to meet people. She decided to sign on to an on-line dating service. During the sign-up process she was presented with something called "The Wife List." This list featured the most desirable qualities in women as reported by men. The seven characteristics given were as follows: (1) attractive; (2) smart; (3) not materialistic; (4) trustworthy; (5) ambitious; (6) selfless; (7) confident.

That same day, John, a twenty-six-year-old accountant from another state, whose life was just as hectic, signed on to the same service. He was introduced to "The Husband List." This list featured the most desirable qualities in men as reported by women. The seven qualities on this list included these: (1) financially secure; (2) faithful; (3) honest; (4) sense of humor; (5) respectful; (6) ambitious; (7) family-oriented.

The interesting thing about this story is not the content of the lists but the fact that there are lists in the first place. One list seeks to highlight virtues that women desire in men in order to help men connect better with women. The other list seeks to highlight virtues that men desire in women in order to help women better connect with men. The thinking is that if we know what is desired and expected of us then we will have greater likelihood of meeting those desires and expectations.

Wouldn't it be nice if God gave believers a list of preferred qualities? Wouldn't it be nice if God highlighted for us the virtues God expects the church to pursue? Good news! He has. Let's turn to Ephesians 4. This lesson is intended to help us identify qualities and actions the church is to demonstrate as Christ's body.

Guide Bible Study

4. Refer to the *Study Guide* and the "Bible Comments" section in this *Teaching Guide* for assistance in understanding, explaining, and clarifying biblical material throughout the lesson.

5. Read Ephesians 4:1–6. Summarize and explain these verses. Direct learners' attention to the lesson handout. (The completed version is provided below for your use.) Instruct learners to write **Calling** in the

first blank under the section "The Church United" (Roman numeral I.). Explain what Paul meant in verse 1 by the phrase "live a life." Ask: *How can we obey this command?* Guide learners to respond to this question by considering the following areas of their lives: spiritual, mental, emotional, physical, social, political, or economic.

Lesson Outline
The Church Fulfilling Its Calling
Ephesians 4:1–16

The church is to live in a manner worthy of its calling as the body of Christ.

 I. The Church United (4:1–6)

  A. Its **Calling** (1)

  B. Its **Characteristics** (2–3)

  C. Its **Common** Denominator (4–6)

 II. The Church Using Gifts (4:7–13)

  A. **Character** of Gifts (7)

  B. Source of Gifts (8–10)

  C. **Identity** of Gifts (11)

  D. **Function** of Gifts (12–13)

 III. The Church Grows Up (4:14–16)

  A. Immaturity (14)

  B. Maturity (15–16)

---

6. Instruct learners to write **Characteristics** in the second blank under this section. Read verse 2. Explain the meaning of "be completely humble." Ask learners to give you specific examples of a time when they have witnessed this virtue demonstrated. Explain "be . . . gentle." Ask learners to give you specific examples of a time when they have witnessed this virtue demonstrated. Explain the meaning of "be patient." Ask learners to give you specific examples of a time when they have witnessed this virtue demonstrated. Explain the meaning of "bearing with one another in love." Ask learners to

give you specific examples of a time when they have witnessed this virtue demonstrated.

7. Read verse 3. Explain how the virtues in verse 2 impact how we maintain unity in the church. Support your thoughts by reading and summarizing Romans 12:18 and Philippians 2:1–5.

8. Instruct learners to write **Common** in the third blank under this section. Ask: *How many times is the idea of "one" mentioned? What does this mean for the church?*

9. Direct learners' attention to the "The Church Using Gifts" section of the handout (Roman numeral II.). Read Ephesians 4:7–13. Instruct learners to write **Character** in the first blank under this section. Explain how Paul used the word "grace" in verse 7. Read 1 Corinthians 12:7 and relate it to Paul's use in Ephesians 4:7. Ask learners to give a specific example of when they have seen the "grace" of God at work in someone's life.

10. Instruct learners to write **Identity** in the second blank under this section. Read verse 11, and explain the various assignments given by Christ.

11. Instruct learners to write **Function** in the third blank under this section. Read verses 12–13, and explain the function and purpose of the various gifts given in verse 11.

12. Read verses 14–16 and describe the differences between immature and mature believers.

Encourage Application

13. Distribute "The Church List" handout. (It is available in "Teaching Resource Items" for this study at www.baptistwaypress.org. The completed list in printed below for your use.) Summarize the lesson.

The Church List
Ephesians 4:1–16

1. *Humility (2)*
2. *Gentleness (2)*
3. *Patience (2)*
4. *Bearing with one another in love (2)*
5. *Unity (3)*
6. *Peaceful (3)*
7. *Service (12)*

---

14. Restate the teaching aim for the lesson.

15. Help learners complete "The Church List" by dictating to them qualities and actions the church is to demonstrate. Be sure to give the Scripture reference for each quality. It may be helpful to reread the verses to help with reinforcing the teaching.

16. Conclude the class session with prayer.

NOTES ——————————————————————————————

1. Unless otherwise indicated, all Scripture quotations in lessons 5–7 and 12–13 are from the New International Version, 1984 edition.

MAIN IDEA
Members of Christ's body are to change their way of living to the way of Christ.

QUESTION TO EXPLORE
To what extent do your daily behaviors reflect the way of Christ?

TEACHING AIM
To lead the class to describe the teachings about Christian living in this passage and to decide to implement the one that is most difficult for them to practice

LESSON SIX
Live the New Way of Christ

BIBLE COMMENTS

Understanding the Context

The application of the first half of the letter continues in this passage. As noted in lesson five, the final three chapters of the Ephesians letter contain Paul's directives for how the church must respond to God's work of love in Christ. After establishing that God shows his overwhelming love for his church through the unparalleled gift of his divine Son, Paul laid out the characteristics of a faithfully responsive church.

Few passages in Scripture instruct more on daily living than what is contained in these condensed verses. One after another, Paul recounted to the recipients of this letter what it meant to live in the light of the love of God. Typical of Pauline material, Paul was most likely responding to real situations involving actual people. Perhaps a messenger had delivered an alarming dispatch to Paul about the discouraging lifestyle of the churches in this area. Maybe Paul had a more direct contact with the church in Ephesus through Timothy (see 1 Timothy 1:3–4), or perhaps Tychicus had made earlier trips to the region (see Ephesians 6:21–22). Regardless of how Paul knew, he was keenly aware of the Ephesian way of life. In response, he was forthright with direct instruction.

This section of the letter is all about change. Each thought calls for a change from one behavior to another, from the way of the world to the way of Christ. As the letter traveled from church to church, believers had to confront the sobering realization that their behavior might well have triggered Paul's remarks. As the eternal nature of Scripture continues to speak to Christians today, contemporary readers find needed changes in their own lives, as well.

Interpreting the Scriptures

Changing from the Former Way of Living to Christ's Way (4:17–32)

4:17–19. As Paul unfolds the list of expectations that describe how Christians "must no longer live as the Gentiles do," the reader should keep in mind that these words are more than a rulebook. His purpose was to describe a life well-lived as an imitator of Christ. Paul did not offer a checklist of conduct, the fulfillment of which leads to pride. Rather, these words describe the life of the believer who is living as Christ taught in response to and gratitude for salvation.

Undeniably, a pagan-infused society maintained a stronghold in Ephesus, in sharp contrast to the Christian culture there. Paul repeatedly called the Christians to live a life distinct from the unbelievers around them. He described those who lived antithetically to the Christian walk, including their untruthful thinking, their stubborn hearts, their impure actions, and their greedy motivations. The way of life in Christ is the opposite of this deceitful life.

4:20–24. Paul exhorted Christians to live the new way of Christ by first reminding them what they already knew. They already knew the way they should live. They knew the way of Christ, and they needed to practice the basics they had learned from the beginning of their faith journey. Paul's assumption is very important to the rest of the passage. To walk with Christ, Christians must learn and embrace the teachings of Christ. The demands of the Christian way are far too high for those who do not have the truth of Christ in their hearts.

Paul's description of putting off the old and putting on the new provides a clear picture for the first-century Christians as well as the faithful today. The old self resembles the life of the Gentiles, which Paul rejected, while the new self ought to look like the life of Christ. Of course, the old must be completely abolished if the new is going to be complete. These words are not about a new coat over old clothes but rather an entirely new set of garments.

4:25–28. This section provides illustrations to cement the imagery. Put off lying, and put on truth-telling. Put off harboring anger (see Psalm 4:4), and put on Godlike control of one's life. Put off stealing, and put on an honest way of life. While the list can certainly be expanded, the brevity of these three examples accentuates Paul's supposition that the readers already knew the right way. Since they had already learned the way of Christ, they knew the difference between the pagan life of the world and the Christian life of the church. These guidelines were not meant to be exhaustive but rather illustrative of the conflicting behaviors that the readers already should have known.

4:29–32. Paul further elaborated on some of the expected behaviors. Not only should the Christian "speak truthfully" (Eph. 4:25), but also the follower of Christ should say only what builds up the other person. How many sentences would go unspoken if they had to pass through this edification filter before being uttered?

Sinful actions sorrow the Holy Spirit. Bad choices go far beyond a failure to edify others; they grieve the very Spirit of God. To make matters worse, the Spirit who grieves because of our sins is the same Spirit whom Christians expect to guarantee their redemption (see 1:13–14).

Returning to the depiction of taking off the old and putting on the new, Paul called for a removal of bitter anger and an embracing of compassionate forgiveness. This challenge, along with many of the others in this passage, might be reasonably expected. However, the distinct underpinning of this new behavior is the action of God through Christ. Forgive, "as in Christ God forgave you" (4:32).

Changing from the Old Darkness to the New Light of Life (5:1–20)

5:1–2. In similar fashion as in the preceding verses, Paul reinforced the motivation of the new behavior to be the actions of God through Christ. The way of Christ is the way of love. The way of love was most completely revealed when Christ "gave himself up for us as a fragrant offering and sacrifice to God."

5:3–7. This section begins and ends with the idea of separateness. Christians are "God's holy people," signifying that they have been set apart from the world's standards and instead called to God's way of living. Toward the end of these verses, Paul admonished the holy ones to avoid partnering with those walking the other way (5:7). The sense of disconnection is deliberate. Christians abandon the old way of life so they can unite with God in the new way. This detachment notwithstanding, the call is to live this new life in the world. Paul did not guide the Ephesians to withdraw from the world but rather to live differently within their culture.

5:8–14. Light is Paul's next metaphor to represent change in the Christian. The comparison of Christ's way to the pagan way is as opposite as light is to darkness. One cannot ignore the similarity of Paul's description to the words of Christ himself: "I am the light of the world. Whoever follows me will never walk in darkness, but will have the light of life" (John 8:12). As one who is asleep wakes up to the light of the sun, so, too, must those who are asleep in their sins awake to the light of Christ.

5:15–20. As this section comes to its conclusion, Paul offered another principle of walking the correct path. Simply put, it is to "be very careful." Once more, the implication is that the Ephesian readers knew the correct way (see comments on Eph. 4:20–24). The suggestion in this verse from Paul was that they needed to pay attention to where they were going.

In their vigilance, they should make the "most of every opportunity." Every moment grants another opportunity to walk as Christ leads. Given that "the days are evil," Christians should not miss a step. The idea of evil days most likely refers to the trouble that each day brings. The sinful pitfalls of this world can make walking the Christian path a great challenge.

Being "drunk on wine" contrasts markedly with being "filled with the Spirit." Putting off drunkenness and putting on a Spirit-filled life further illustrates Paul's engaging imagery in this passage. Appropriately, this lesson closes in worship. With singing and thanksgiving, the Christian can find culmination in joy before God in worship.

Focusing on the Meaning

Several overarching truths accompany applying this passage to the contemporary Christian walk. First, we must accept that these behaviors occur in the world—where we work, play, and worship. This passage does not suggest that Christians separate themselves from the world to live this new life. The Christ-like walk treks intentionally through our places of employment, our homes, our neighborhoods, and our churches. The conflict of living as a Christian in a non-Christian world often tempts us to dismiss Paul's words. However, we cannot overlook the power of our witness when we live our faith in the presence of those who do not believe.

Additionally, we must recognize that new conduct requires removal of the old. Consider which of the teachings in the passage might be the most challenging to put into action. To change, to implement one of these new practices, we must consciously commit to stop the old way. What happens if someone puts on a fresh suit after a long day of working in the yard but fails to remove the old clothes first? This same scenario occurs when faithful people try to walk two paths, one that follows Christ and one that does not.

Finally, do not ignore the significance that the passage ends with praise and thanksgiving toward God. The challenge of Paul may sound daunting, but the result will be rejoicing. The new way of Christ leads to celebration of faith before God with others who have committed to the same walk.

TEACHING PLANS

Teaching Plan—Varied Learning Activities

Connect with Life

1. Prior to class beginning, place a copy of the lesson handout, "Do's & Don'ts," at each learner's place. The lesson handout is available in "Teaching Resource Items" for this study at www.baptistwaypress.org.

2. Begin the class with a triangle prayer exercise. Ask learners to get into groups of three people each. Direct learners to listen to your instructions before they take any action. Instruct learners to:
    a. Share a specific request for prayer
    b. Pray for each member's prayer request
    c. Take about seven minutes total for this time of prayer
    d. Stop praying when they hear you start praying
    e. Begin praying

3. At the seven-minute mark, pray for God's blessing for this lesson.

4. Lead the class in a discussion regarding how we use lists in our culture. Comment that using lists is how we tend to do life. Call for examples of lists (such as to-do list, grocery list, Christmas list, best-seller list, Billboard Top 100, David Letterman's Top 10 List). Then ask: *Why do we use lists?* Summarize the various thoughts learners offer.

5. Inform learners that in this lesson we are going to look at a few lists of biblical instructions.

Guide Bible Study

6. Refer to the *Study Guide* and the "Bible Comments" section in this *Teaching Guide* for assistance in understanding, explaining, and clarifying biblical material throughout the lesson.

7. Direct learners to gather in groups of three or four members each. Assign each group one of the following passages: (1) Ephesians 4:17–32; (2) Ephesians 5:1–7; (3) Ephesians 5:8–14; (4) Ephesians 5:15–20.

8. Instruct groups to review their assigned passage and list its do's and don'ts on the lesson handout. After they have completed their lists, instruct groups to discuss answers to the following questions: *What does the passage teach you about God? What does the passage teach you about people? What does the passage teach you about life in general?* In other words, you are asking what does this passage teach about how God thinks, feels, and acts, as well as about how people tend to think, feel and act. Also you're asking what this passage teaches about how life tends to work.

9. Direct learners to select a group representative who will report to the class their list of do's and don'ts. If there is more than one group with the same passage, then allow one group to report and the other group or groups to make additions.

10. Allow groups to report on their lists. After each report, lead the class in guided discussion asking the following questions: *What should we learn from this list? What prevents us from adhering to these lessons?*

Encourage Application

11. Instruct learners to disperse from their groups.

12. Summarize the lesson by using information in "Focusing on the Meaning" in this *Teaching Guide* and "Putting Faith into Practice" in the *Study Guide.*

13. Prepare and distribute the "Spiritual Work Order" handout. A copy is available in "Teaching Resource Items" for this study at www.baptistwaypress.org. Explain to learners that a work order is a request for service.

Spiritual Work Order

Your Name: _____

Today's Date: _____

Time: _____

Describe the teaching from this lesson that you find most difficult to embrace (accept and obey).

In light of today's lesson, what will you do in the next seven days to address the challenge you described above?

---

14. Inform learners that you are going to give them five minutes to complete their Spiritual Work Order.

15. End the session by praying God's grace on learners to complete the work they have committed to do.

Teaching Plan—Lecture and Questions

Connect with Life

1. Call for a volunteer to lead the class in prayer.

2. Use the illustration "Read the Instructions" to begin the lesson.

Read the Instructions

Ray was a college senior studying at a large university in California. This was his final year of school but his first year of living off campus. He was finally going to have his own place. This meant no more roommates, no more sharing restrooms with twenty other people, and most importantly, no more on-campus curfews.

Excited about his new life, Ray went to a store to purchase a modern home entertainment center for his television and other electronic equipment. He found just what he wanted. Its dimensions were impressive. It was sixty-five inches high by seventy-eight inches wide by seventeen inches deep. It could accommodate a forty-five-inch flat screen television. It had an open storage for AV equipment and his PlayStation console. It had reversible back panels and open storage shelves on either side to keep DVDs and other items. It was exactly want he wanted. But there was some hesitation on Ray's part. You see, the box was marked with those dreaded words, "some assembly required."

Ray made the purchase anyway. He was so excited that he rushed to his apartment and started on his new project. He opened the box, pulled out equipment and materials, and began to assemble his entertainment center. After two hours or so, Ray was through with his project. But there was a problem. The entertainment center that Ray assembled didn't look anything like the picture on the box. As a matter of fact there were some leftover screws, tacks, and even a shelf that he did not know what to do with. He called a friend for advice. His friend asked, "Did you read the instructions?" There was silence. His friend interjected, "Dude, you should have read the instructions."

Ray disregarded the manufacturer's right to instruct him on how to handle their product in order for him to get the maximum enjoyment and benefit. As Christians we are the "products" of God's work of salvation (Eph. 2:10). He created our salvation. Sadly, we don't always get the maximum benefit and enjoyment from our salvation experience because too many times we disregard God's instruction on how to live the Christian life.

This Bible study lesson highlights God's right to instruct believers and our responsibility to live in obedience to God's instructions.

3. Refer to the Study Aim in the *Study Guide,* and encourage learners to keep it in mind: "To describe the teachings about Christian living in this passage and to decide to implement the one that is most difficult for me to practice."

Guide Bible Study

4. Refer to the *Study Guide* and the "Bible Comments" section in this *Teaching Guide* for assistance in understanding, explaining, and clarifying biblical material throughout the lesson.

5. Read Ephesians 4:17–24. Summarize these verses. Explain how Paul described the Gentiles (4:17–19). Emphasize the need for Christians to live differently than ungodly cultures live. Ask: *What are some of the ways that Christians fail to be different from our culture?*

6. Discuss Paul's clothing metaphor in 4:24–25. Explore how Romans 12:1–3 relates to Paul's instructions in these verses.

7. Read Ephesians 4:25–32. Summarize the passage. Reread verse 26. Ask: *How can you be angry and not sin?*

8. Reread verse 28. Ask: *What did Paul give as his purpose for commanding the one who steals to stop stealing? What does this teach you about the heart of God? about the Christian life?*

9. Reread verse 30. Ask: *What does it mean to "grieve the Holy Spirit"? What does this look like today?* Be prepared to make clarifications where needed.

10. Reread verse 31. Ask: *What does it mean to forgive others as God has forgiven us?* Ask learners to give a specific examples for support.

11. Read Ephesians 5:1–7. Explain Paul's use of the phrase "imitators of God." Call for specific examples. Invite comments on how verse 3 applies to our current culture.

12. Read Ephesians 5:8–14. Summarize the passage. Explore how these verses might apply to the various areas of learners' lives (mental, emotional, spiritual, physical, social).

13. Read Ephesians 5:15–20. Summarize the passage. Explain what it means to be "filled with the Spirit" (5:18). Be prepared to make clarifications where needed.

Encourage Application

14. Inform learners that you are going to give them two minutes to list three of the teachings in this passage that are most difficult for them. By "difficult" we mean our individual inability or challenge to embrace and obey the teaching. Inform them that this is not a group assignment and that they will work quietly and alone.

15. After two minutes, instruct learners to circle the teaching that is most difficult for them to accept or obey. Instruct learners to write down what they can do during the next seven days to put that teaching into practice.

16. Conclude the session by praying God's strength and power for learners to be faithful to God's instructions.

FOCAL TEXT
Ephesians 5:21—6:9

BACKGROUND
Ephesians 5:21—6:9

MAIN IDEA
All relationships in the
Christian household are to be
ordered by reverence for Christ.

QUESTION TO EXPLORE
How does Christian faith
affect relationships at home
and at work—or does it?

TEACHING AIM
To help the class describe
differences that would result
if they ordered their home
and work relationships
by reverence for Christ

LESSON SEVEN
*Life in a
Christian
Household*

BIBLE COMMENTS

Understanding the Context

One of the basic steps in proper biblical interpretation is to consider the context within which a passage was written. Context helps to address this question: What did the passage originally mean to the people who first read it? The verses in this lesson are certainly no exception to this important principle. To understand what this Scripture passage means today, we need to grasp its significance in the first-century world.

Toward that end, we note that the first readers of this letter were keenly aware of similar teachings outside of their Christian circles. The majority of the ideas in this passage were not necessarily unique demands to the Christian faith, and so their non-Christian friends would not find many of these words unusual. Certain expectations of relationships— between spouses, between parents and children, and between slaves and masters—were common to many sets of instructions in the first-century Greco-Roman world. This connection is important given the fact that Paul has just completed a large section in this letter on how Christians must walk the way of Christ while remaining in the world (see lesson six). This lesson further strengthens his case as he emphasized how the Christian faith affects the relationships that exist in the household.

Ephesians 5:22—6:9 is sometimes spoken of as a household or station code. The concept refers to these household relationships as life stations in the first century. Other such codes can be found in Colossians 3:18—4:1; Titus 2:1–10; and 1 Peter 2:18—3:7.

Interpreting the Scriptures

Husbands and Wives in the Christian Household (5:21–33)

5:21. Many of your group members may have Bible translations that place this verse in a preceding section. Such a position naturally gives the impression that this verse is somewhat separated thematically and biblically from Ephesians 5:22 and following. Be careful in allowing section titles in various translations to dictate the connection between

verses. This keynote verse is actually the beginning to a proper understanding of the entire passage that follows.

Significantly, "submit" is actually a participle, as in *submitting*. It
joins a line of participles stretching through the previous verses. These
participles refer to the actions of *speaking* (Ephesians 5:19), *singing* (Eph.
5:19), *making music* (5:19), and "giving thanks" (5:20). Each of these participles, including the idea of submitting in this verse, refers back to the
imperative, "be filled with the Spirit" (5:18). When the Christian speaks,
sings, makes music, gives thanks, and submits, she or he is responding
to the filling of the Spirit. As the remainder of this passage develops the
idea of submitting to one another, such submission actually begins with
being "filled with the Spirit" (5:18).

In the time of Paul's writing, the concept of submission referred
mostly to the already accepted order of relationships. For instance,
when the word was used in a military context, it denoted the structured
arrangement of the troops under the command of a designated leader.
In all relationships, a hierarchy was viewed as essential so that the society as a whole could function in an orderly fashion. As Paul articulated
these principles for the Christian household, he would have been aware
that this pattern was already embedded in the Greco-Roman culture of
the first century.

Today's contemporary Bible student must understand that the larger
social order was considered to be built off of the smaller, household
order. This building-block structure of the passage also gives the passage
meaning for those who are not married or who may not have children.
The idea is that all individual relationships are important because they
impact society as a collective whole.

5:22–33. The remainder of this passage provides examples of how
people within the Christian household ought to "submit to one another
out of reverence for Christ" (5:21). In each of the household relationships, the pattern for the Christian to follow should flow out of the
predominant "reverence for Christ" (5:21). This reverence is constructed
from awe and respect for Christ, which was described and developed
throughout the first sections of this Letter to the Ephesians. The lavish-
ness of God through Christ (lesson one), the unity of the church through
Christ (lesson three), and the dwelling of Christ's love in the mission of
the church (lesson four) are a few of the qualities that call for reverence
of Christ.

This section focuses on the husband-and-wife relationship. The underlying concept of this passage is that whenever submission is mentioned, it underscores the earlier view of submitting to one another (5:21). Too often misunderstood and misused, this passage can be properly appreciated by keeping uppermost the thought of husband and wife submitting to one another as the primary understanding. A phrase such as "head of the wife" might be dangerous indeed if it were isolated out of the text. Instead, the phrase must be interpreted as mutual submission to one another out of a deep reverence for Christ. "Head of the wife' is placed within a relationship in which the husband submits to the wife and the wife submits to the husband. Submission to each other as husband and wife is an example of how Christians live out their faith in the home; after all, the family is an example of how "Christ loved the church."

Parents and Children in the Christian Household (6:1–4)

The next familial relationship that Paul considered was that of parents and their children. Paul appealed to the commandment: "Honor your father and your mother, so that you may live long in the land the LORD your God is giving you" (Exodus 20:12). The command comes with a result, a promise that reveals the value of order in the parent-and-child relationship. From the parents, the child learns his or her part in God's calling of his children to the land that he promised them.

Perhaps sensing the need to remind parents of the Christian context of his words, Paul instructed the fathers specifically not to "exasperate your children." The admonition was to refrain from provoking their children to anger. Instead, parents should rear their children under the teachings of Christ. Once more, the context always returns to how the Christian household is ordered from an outpouring of "reverence for Christ" (Eph. 5:21).

Slaves and Master in the Christian Household (6:5–9)

6:5–8. Readers today struggle with a passage that begins with "slaves, obey your earthly masters" (6:5). Clearly, this verse could add fuel to the flames of those who might seek biblical support for the institution of slavery. This section serves as a good example of how context is important in the interpretation of Scripture. The relationship between slave and master, while part of the world in which Paul lived, serves as an illustration of the order in Paul's day. In light of Paul's comment in Galatians (Galatians 3:28) that removed the distinction between slave and free, this Ephesians passage can only be a descriptive illustration of order in Paul's day, instead of a prescription for continued slave-and-master relationships.

6:9. Paul came just shy of denouncing slavery himself in this very passage. When he returned to the idea of submitting to one another, he called for masters to "treat your slaves in the same way." Not only was Paul guiding slaves to relate to masters with "respect and fear, and with sincerity of heart;" (6:5) but he was also calling for masters to act in the "same way" as the Lord. The Lord will reward a person, "whether he is slave or free" (6:8). Paul challenged the first-century Christians to recognize that Christ makes no distinction.

Consider this passage as guidance applicable to employee and employer relationships. With that association as the backdrop, the instruction is a useful tool in establishing yet another relationship in "reverence for Christ" (5:21).

Focusing on the Meaning

The contemporary lesson from this Ephesian household code is the ordering of relationships at home or work out of "reverence for Christ" (5:21). Rather than approaching the passage with an out-of-context attempt to validate certain theological positions, instead apply this passage to primary relationships of life. The guides in these household instructions should strengthen today's relationships, just as in Paul's day.

Since the basic tenet of the household code defined by Paul was order, center on that truth as the essential guide for today. Household codes give order to the most basic of relationships. According to Paul, this order always begins with Christ. Since "reverence for Christ" (5:21) is the primary focus, any order in a relationship must have Christ at its center. Without Christ, the primary emphasis of the order is absent.

As students consider their various relationships as in the Scriptures, encourage them first to consider whether Christ is at the center. If Christ is at the core of the relationship, then the next step of mutual submission to each other is natural and fitting. Finally, delve into the idea of what might change in the family, at work, in church, or in the world, if relationships were centered on Christ with the outgrowth of that faith being submission to one another.

TEACHING PLANS

Teaching Plan—Varied Learning Activities

Connect with Life

1. Prior to class beginning, place a blank index card in each learner's chair.

2. Begin the class with a partnering-in-prayer exercise. Direct learners to listen to your instructions before they take any action. Instruct learners to
   a. Get physically next to another learner with whom they have never prayed
   b. Share a specific request for prayer
   c. Allow the partner to pray for him or her and the learner in turn to pray for the specific request of the partner
   d. Take about five-to-seven minutes total for this time of prayer
   e. Stop praying when they hear you start praying
   f. Begin praying

3. At the five-to-seven minute mark, pray for God's blessing for this lesson.

4. Instruct learners to close their eyes. Instruct them to think about their home and work life (What's going well? What's not going so well? Why?). Instruct learners to open their eyes. Direct learners to write on their blank index card a challenge, problem, or issue they

are having in their home or work life. Emphasize that this is for their private use only.

Guide Bible Study

5. Refer to the *Study Guide* and the "Bible Comments" section in this *Teaching Guide* for assistance in understanding, explaining, and clarifying biblical material throughout the lesson.

6. Direct learners to gather in groups of three or four members. Enlist a volunteer to read Ephesians 5:21–24. Instruct groups to discuss the meaning of the word "submit" as well as why wives are commanded to do so.

7. Enlist a volunteer to read Ephesians 5:25–29. Direct groups to discuss answers to these questions: *How are husbands commanded to love their wives? How is the husband to accomplish this?*

8. Invite a volunteer to read Ephesians 6:1–4. Instruct groups to discuss the potential results in family life if children and parents embraced the teachings of this passage.

9. Have a volunteer read Ephesians 6:5–9. Instruct groups to answer this question: *What are the potential results in the work place if employers and employees practiced the teachings of this passage?*

10. Direct groups to discuss answers to this question: *How does Christ factor into the commands of the teachings of Ephesians 5:21—6:9?*

11. Distribute the "7 Hearts" handout. Review the instructions with learners. The handout is available in "Teaching Resource Items" for this study at www.baptistwaypress.org. Allow ten minutes or so for this group exercise, and then receive reports.

---

7 Hearts
Ephesians 5:21—6:9

The teachings of the Apostle Paul in this lesson were addressed to seven groups of people. His commands to each group called for them to embrace a particular attitude or heart condition.

In the word game below, view the seven people groups Paul addressed in the left column and determine a word or phrase that represents the attitude or heart condition that Paul desired for that particular group. Write the correct word or words in the spaces provided. You may refer to your Bible for assistance.

People   **Hearts**

1. Children   _____

2. Husbands   _____

3. Masters   _____

4. All   _____

5. Fathers   _____

6. Slaves   _____

7. Wives   _____

Encourage Application

12. Direct learners to disperse from their groups.

13. Ask learners to review the index card on which they recorded their personal challenge, issue, or problem. Instruct them to review the heart conditions displayed in the word game. Ask: *How might things be different if you adopted one of the seven heart conditions?* Direct learners to write their response on the blank side of the index card.

14. End the session by asking God to give each learner the strength for faithfulness.

Teaching Plan—Lecture and Questions

Connect with Life

1. Prior to class beginning, place a copy of the lesson handout in the chair of each learner. The lesson handout is the partially completed outline of the lesson. Learners will fill in the blanks on the lesson handout as you teach the lesson. The lesson handout as well as a completed lesson outline (to be used by you to guide learners through the lesson) is available in "Teaching Resource Items" for this study at www.baptistwaypress.org.

Lesson Handout
Life in a Christian Household
Ephesians 5:21—6:9

All relationships in the Christian household are to be ordered by reverence for Christ.

  I. The Guiding Principle (5:21)

  II. Husbands and Wives (5:22–33)

    A. Responsibilities of _____ (22–24)

    B. Responsibilities of _____ (25–33)

  III. Children and Parents (6:1–4)

    A. Responsibilities of _____ (1–3)

    B. Responsibilities of _____ (4)

  IV. Slaves and Masters (6:5–9)

    A. Responsibilities of _____ (6–8)

    B. Responsibilities of _____ (9)

Completed Lesson Outline
Life in a Christian Household
Ephesians 5:21—6:9

All relationships in the Christian household are to be ordered by reverence for Christ.

I. The Guiding Principle (5:21)

II. Husbands and Wives (5:22–33)
   A. Responsibilities of **Wives** (22–24)
   B. Responsibilities of **Husbands** (25–33)

III. Children and Parents (6:1–4)
   A. Responsibilities of **Children** (1–3)
   B. Responsibilities of **Fathers** (4)

IV. Slaves and Masters (6:5–9)
   A. Responsibilities of **Slaves** (6–8)
   B. Responsibilities of **Masters** (9)

---

2. Begin class by asking for praise reports regarding those who were able to faithfully carry out the application of lesson six. Review the application as needed. Thank God in prayer for these learners and pray for those who are still pursuing their commitments.

3. Instruct learners to close their eyes. Tell them to think about their lives, especially their home life and work life. Tell them to think about the good, the bad, and the ugly parts of their lives. While their eyes are still closed, ask rhetorically, *Wouldn't you like to keep the good stuff and change the bad stuff?* Inform them that in this lesson they are going to see how their walk with Jesus can affect relationships at home and at work. Instruct learners to open their eyes. Allow about three-to-five minutes for this exercise.

Guide Bible Study

4. Refer to the *Study Guide* and the "Bible Comments" section in this *Teaching Guide* for assistance in understanding, explaining, and clarifying biblical material throughout the lesson.

5. Direct learners' attention to the lesson handout (see step 1). Read Ephesians 5:21. Define the word "submit." Explain how this verse relates to the rest of the passages within the lesson. Ask learners to share their thoughts on what Paul meant by the phrase "out of reverence for Christ."

6. Instruct learners to write **Wives** in the first blank under the "Husbands and Wives" section of their handout. Read Ephesians 5:22–24. Explain these verses using information in the *Study Guide* and "Bible Comments" in this *Teaching Guide*. Instruct learners to write **Husbands** in the second blank of this section. Read verses 25–33. Explain these verses using information in the *Study Guide* and "Bible Comments" in this *Teaching Guide*. Summarize the passage. Refer to Colossians 3:18–19 also.

7. Ask learners these questions: *How does the current American culture challenge the roles of husbands and wives? For those of you who are married or have been married, if you could replay your roles, what would you do differently?*

8. Read Ephesians 6:1–4. Instruct learners to write **Children** in the first blank under the section "Children and Parents." Explain the role of children in family life. Refer to Colossians 3:20 also. Ask learners these questions: *How does the culture affect children's ability to obey the instructions of Scripture? What can the church do to help? How can parents help?*

9. Instruct learners to write **Fathers** in the second blank under this section. Explain the responsibilities of the father in home life. Refer to Colossians 3:21. Ask: *How does our current culture help or hinder fathers in obeying this teaching? What changes do fathers need to make?*

10. Read Ephesians 6:5–9. Instruct learners to write **Slaves** in the first blank under the "Slaves and Masters" section. Instruct learns to write

Masters in the second blank. Explain the responsibilities of slaves and masters according to these verses. Refer to Colossians 3:22—4:1 for support. Ask: *How do you think Paul's teachings in these verses apply in the American work place? What kind of impact could these teachings have on your work environment? Why? Why not?*

Encourage Application

11. Lead learners in a discussion of this question: *What differences would result if you ordered your home and work relationships according to Paul's teachings in this passage?*

12. Conclude the session with prayer.

FOCAL TEXT
1 Timothy 1:1–5, 12–19

BACKGROUND
1 Timothy 1

MAIN IDEA
Paul's experience of God's grace and mercy shaped his life, his ministry, and his message, and provided an example of leadership and service for Timothy.

QUESTIONS TO EXPLORE
Who has provided for you a positive example of Christian leadership and service? How are you providing such an example to others?

TEACHING AIM
To lead adults to identify qualities of Paul that provide an example of Christian leadership and service worth following

LESSON EIGHT
An Example to Follow

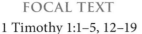

BIBLE COMMENTS

Understanding the Context

At turning points or stress points in our lives we may need mentors to help us. Such was the case of Paul for Timothy. First Timothy presents a situation in which Timothy and Paul had ministered together in Ephesus. Paul then left Timothy behind and most likely moved on to Macedonia, leaving Timothy to shepherd the church at Ephesus. He did not forget Timothy. He knew the church and situation well and knew his young fellow missionary needed encouragement. Paul addressed Timothy, the church leaders, and the church through this first letter.

Think of having thrust upon you responsibilities you feel ill-equipped to meet. While Timothy was an experienced missionary, he had different kinds of responsibilities with the church at Ephesus. Ephesus was no easy place to build and sustain a community of believers. As it was an important trade center, it became a melting pot of cultures and religious loyalties. The worship of Artemis flourished there. Artemis was a fertility or nature goddess for whom the Ephesians built an impressive temple. Magic, superstitions, and strands of different philosophies occupied the attention of some. Timothy had administrative challenges, moral challenges, and doctrinal challenges to and within the church in that context. Paul's help and example encouraged Timothy to be steadfast in his ministry.

First Timothy is not an extensive *how-to* book. It does contain some administrative and organizational details, but Paul trusted his young colleague to work out the details from his commitment to Jesus. He supported Timothy as Timothy faced difficult issues. He did expect Timothy to carefully gather around him fellow Christians of doctrinal soundness and moral conduct to help meet the challenges. Some of Paul's strongest encouragement came at points of Christian faith and practice in the face of the challenges. As Timothy read the letter, he heard the words from a mentor who was his example, a person who backed up his words by the life he lived and the leadership he provided.[1]

Interpreting the Scriptures

The Example Source (1:1–2)

1:1. The sender of the letter in those times commonly named himself first, followed by the recipient or recipients, a greeting, the body of the letter, and a conclusion. The conclusion often was an additional greeting or benediction. We notice that Paul *Christianized* this form. His identity as sender was more than his name but was descriptive, as was Timothy's identity as recipient. "Grace . . . and peace," again a common letter greeting in that day, was more as well, as it was "grace, mercy, and peace from God the Father and Christ Jesus our Lord."

Thus, Paul was not just Paul; he was a person under command. As an apostle (one who is sent) he had the responsibility of so well representing the one sending him that it was as if the one sending him was there. Neither time nor space prevented Jesus from working through Paul. Jesus and "God our Savior," the commander of all, sent Paul as an apostle. The apostleship and command were present realities to Paul, growing out of a living relationship with God the Father and the Son. The term "Savior" applied to both Jesus and God. Jesus as the "hope" was not an exercise in possibility thinking but a certainty. Paul, Timothy, and the church lived toward the fulfillment of all the promises in Christ, which nothing could ultimately deny. In this opening testimony we witness the heart of Paul from which flowed his example and life.

1:2. Timothy was a pivotal fellow missionary with Paul. Acts 16:1–3 tells us that Timothy was a native of Lystra, that his father was Greek and his mother Jewish, that he had a strong reputation as a believer, and that Paul wanted Timothy to go with him on mission. Paul affirmed Timothy in Philippians 2:22 as an effective missionary and characterized their closeness as that of a father to a son. Paul apparently sent Timothy to Philippi to encourage the church while Paul was in prison. In 1 Corinthians 4:17, Paul announced to the troubled church at Corinth that Timothy was his representative to them, and he exhorted them to treat Timothy with respect (1 Corinthians 16:10). Paul and Timothy were an effective mission team in their work with the early churches. Paul was a mentor, an example, for his young missionary associate as they both served Jesus and the church.

An Example by Life and Words (1:3–4)

1:3. The young congregations of faith were especially vulnerable. They often were dependent on traveling missionaries and teachers for instruction and information. A traveling philosopher or teacher might represent himself to the church for their benefit and actually lead the church in the wrong direction. Sometimes, new members brought teachings from their previous life outside of Christ and tried to adapt Christ to the teachings. The church required Timothy's protection and instruction; they needed him as an example. Thus, Paul urged Timothy on in this vital ministry.

1:4. We see the problem immediately as recorded in this verse, but who was teaching about myths and genealogies and what the myths and genealogies were calls for discussion. One suggestion is related to Gnosticism (from *gnosis,* meaning *knowledge).* Gnosticism was a developing philosophy in the last half of the first century, and it took more concrete shape in the second century. If this philosophy were the source of the "myths," then "myths" may refer to the notion of emanations or beings put out from God, which became more evil with each emanation. In this view, all creation is infected with evil since evil emanations ultimately resulted in an evil creation so that all matter is evil. Spirit, which was good, was locked in evil matter, but with the proper knowledge a person's spirit could be liberated ultimately to make its way back to God. "Genealogies," however, refers more to a Jewish concern than a Gnostic concern. While we cannot be certain about the threatened heresy, some interpreters see it as Judaism entangled with Greek philosophical speculation being brought into the church. It threatened to cloud church members' relationship with Christ, a relationship with God in and through their relationship with Jesus. Followers being threatened by these errors were in need of "divine training," a training referring to right conduct in a faith relationship with Jesus.

1:5. Whatever the exact description of the heresy, Timothy was to be the church instructor and example for sound teaching. He was to do so in a healthy and winsome way. His instruction was to come from "love." "Love" suggests that Timothy's motivation was to be for the redemption of those mistaken, not simply to prove them wrong. "Pure" can refer to unmixed metal where the impurities have been burned away and the true metal is left. Timothy was not, therefore, to harbor any hidden agenda or engage in manipulative behavior to achieve his own goals. "A good conscience" indicates the inherent capacity to determine right and wrong. A "sincere faith" is one in which the way one lives corresponds to what one professes. Paul in his own life was an example of these qualities to Timothy.

An Example in Humility (1:12–17)

1:12–14. Paul never got over or beyond the fact that when he was as far away from Christ Jesus as a person could be that Christ Jesus had accepted him. Indeed, that Jesus would even call Paul to service since he blasphemed God, persecuted the people of Jesus, and was a violent man was utterly remarkable. Paul thought of himself as doing right before he met the resurrected Jesus (see Acts 9:1–9). Just when Christ should have totally rejected him, Christ had "mercy" on him. Mercy is brought into bold relief when this avowed enemy set against Jesus with all that he had available to him was treated as an accepted friend. Paul was a good example to Timothy in sharing out of his own experience and pointing to the "faith and love" in Jesus as a basis for ministry.

1:15–17. Paul was "foremost" in two ways. First, he placed himself at the front of a line as the number one sinner (1 Timothy 1:15). Anyone who thought herself or himself the greatest sinner ran into an objection from Paul. His humility was apparent at this point. He felt himself privileged by grace rather than by his accomplishments. Hence, the statement without any doubt that Christ "came into the world to save sinners" was fitting for Paul's life and any life. Second, since as a great sinner he had been saved by the grace and mercy of Christ, he was a "foremost" example for everyone else (1 Tim. 1:16). If Jesus could and would save Paul, Jesus could and would save any sinner who turned to him. It is not surprising that at this point Paul broke out into doxology, worshiping the One to whom glory and honor belong "forever and ever" (1:17). Again, Paul's own experience became an example for Timothy.

1:18–19. In this section Paul echoed previous words (1:5) as he continued his charge of responsibility to Timothy. His statements are couched in military language. The word translated "instructions" carries the sense of urgent responsibilities, almost a command, so Timothy could "fight the good fight." His weapons were to be "faith and a good conscience." Hence, a strong faith leads to good moral behavior, and a flawed faith leads to bad moral behavior. On the other hand not giving commitment to moral behavior makes a "shipwreck in the faith." Paul had confidence that Timothy was the kind of example in faith and conscience that he should be since Paul earlier had received such good "prophecies" about Timothy concerning Timothy's previous conduct. Timothy knew that Paul's "faith and a good conscience" was not a "shipwreck."

Focusing on the Meaning

Paul was an example because he was a witness to Jesus by his life. Being an example is a by-product of that to which one aspires. A football player so much admired his teammate that he adopted his walk, his stance, and his facial expressions. Others remarked about his conduct, pointing out his likeness to the one he admired. Of course, one football player cannot live in another as Jesus is in us and we are in Jesus. We do not know how Jesus walked and stood, or his facial mannerisms, but we do know about his trust in the Father, his grace, his love, his self-giving, and his moral excellence in every way. Not to take anything away from Paul as regards his commitment to faith and conscience, but Paul's example ultimately depended on his relationship to Jesus.

We do need guidance and encouragement from others, nonetheless. This is one reason Jesus gives us the church. Lone-ranger discipleship leads to self-indulgence and self-dependence. Vital "faith" and a "good conscience" come from relationships to family, friends, and ultimately the church. We need the church teaching right and living right. We need the church's (members') example. We need to be *Pauls* and to have *Pauls* around us.

Reviewing Paul's high regard for Timothy indicates that Timothy also was an encouraging example to Paul. We always receive as well as give. One of the impressive things about Paul that comes through was his deep appreciation for his young fellow missionary. Paul trusted Timothy, which is another aspect of Paul's exampled influence. Good examples are both trustworthy and trusting. People who are examples care. They love with Christ's love. Hence, we are back to the faith relationship and moral conduct distinctives that belong to the authentic example.

TEACHING PLANS

Teaching Plan—Varied Learning Activities

Connect with Life

1. Create a simple unit visual to help learners stay focused during this six-lesson study of 1 and 2 Timothy. One idea: Copy pictures of your church family's recent activities from your church newsletter. Glue these as a collage on poster board. Print the unit title, "1 and 2 Timothy: Leading the Church," on colorful paper and overlay it in the center of the pictures. (Alternate plan: Bring the components and invite early comers to help you assemble the unit visual.)

2. Enlist someone to present this reading as a costumed monologue, a video recording, or a voice from the back of the room. (A copy of the monologue is available in "Teaching Resource Items" for this study at www.baptistwaypress.org.)

A Message from the Apostle Paul

Today I must write to Timothy, my dear son in the faith, my partner, my friend. He is an amazing young man, and I wish you could know him.

About a dozen years ago God brought us together. At the time, Silas and I knew we needed him to help us on our journey west. He was young and strong, and the road ahead would be difficult. We had no idea how much we would need him, but God knew, and I am so grateful for God's provision.

It was during my second mission to Lystra in central Asia that we met Timothy and his family—his godly grandmother, Lois, and mother, Eunice, and also his father who was not of our faith. We had been looking for a younger assistant, and several people suggested that Timothy could be just who we needed. With tears, his family let him go, not knowing where the road would lead.

But God's Spirit knew, and after adding our physician friend Luke to the team, we sailed across the Aegean, landing in Macedonia. Quite an adventure for young Timothy, helping start new churches, seeing us beaten and thrown in prison, being chased out of Macedonia south into Greece, barely escaping plots to kill us. But Timothy proved to be strong, and in time he went with us back to Jerusalem, and later even to Rome.

We have been through much together, Timothy, God, and I: travels, shipwrecks, imprisonments, trials before rulers and even Caesar. So, when a trustworthy person was needed to lead the church in Ephesus and to deal with the false teachers there, Timothy was God's choice. I miss him deeply, but he is too valuable for me to keep to myself.

I hope someday you will meet him. But now, please excuse me—I must begin this letter to my son. There are things I need to tell him.

3. State the Main Idea and raise the Questions to Explore at the beginning of this lesson.

Guide Bible Study

4. Divide the group, and give one research assignment to each half. If attendance is large, suggest smaller huddles of five or six people within each assignment team so that everyone can participate. Allot five to seven minutes for research. (A copy of the assignments is available in "Teaching Resource Items" for this study at www.baptistwaypress.org.)

Team One: Research Timothy's Story
Background Passage: 1 Timothy 1:1–5
Assignment: Using facts from Acts 16:1–5 and Bible maps of Paul's second missionary journey and journey to Rome, illustrate the extensive travels Paul and Timothy shared from A.D. 50 to 62. Point out the beginning place, Lystra in Asia Minor. Also show Macedonia, Greece, Jerusalem, and Rome.

Team Two: Research Paul's Background
Background Passage: 1 Timothy 1:12–17
Assignment: Using Acts 7:57 to 8:3 and Acts 9:1–6, recall the story of Paul's part in the martyrdom of Stephen and in the persecution of the early church. Explain why Paul was *a man with a past*.

5. Call for Team One to read their background passage and present Timothy's story. Affirm their work, and enrich with material from the *Study Guide* section, "Paul Was Courageous in the Face of Opposition (1:3, 18–19)," and from the small article, "Timothy." Emphasize Paul's motivation in 1 Timothy 1:5.

6. Call for Team Two to read their background passage and present Paul's back story. Affirm their work, and follow with additional material from the *Study Guide* section, "Paul Was Convinced of His Salvation (1:12–17)." Summarize Paul's call for integrity in ministry as shown in 1 Timothy 1:18–19.

Encourage Application

7. Distribute sticky pad sheets or note cards. Ask the group to list qualities of leadership they have discovered in the Apostle Paul. (Consider these: he shared leadership, mentored younger associates, built loving relationships, admitted when he was wrong, learned from his mistakes, believed totally in Jesus as Savior and Lord, and was a person of integrity.) Challenge members to keep the list in their Bibles as a reminder of the kind of leaders we can become.

Teaching Plan—Lecture and Questions

Connect with Life

1. Introduce this study, "1 and 2 Timothy: Leading the Church," by reviewing the things these books have in common with the Ephesians study just completed.
   - All three books were written by the Apostle Paul.
   - All three relate to Ephesus: Ephesians was sent directly to them, and Timothy is known to have been pastor of that church (1 Timothy 1:3–4).
   - All three letters deal with the church and church leaders.

2. Invite the group to name people in their experience who have been role models for church leadership. State the Study Aim for this lesson.

Guide Bible Study

3. List four large *C*s on the board. As the study progresses, build this outline for the group to follow:

   C – Confident, 1 Timothy 1:1–2
   C – Courageous, 1 Timothy 1:3–4, 18–19
   C – Compassionate, 1 Timothy 1:5
   C – Convinced, 1 Timothy 1:12–17

4. Invite someone to read 1 Timothy 1:1–2 as you fill in the first *C*, Confident. Lead the group to identify from the verses why Paul felt confident in his calling. Invite volunteers to share what they remember about Paul's conversion and call to the Gentiles (see Acts 9:1–16).

5. Call on a member to read 1 Timothy 1:3–4 as you fill in the second *C*, Courageous. Lead members to name the kind of opposition Timothy could expect. Share details from the *Study Guide* section, "Paul Was Courageous in the Face of Opposition (1:3, 18–19)."

6. Complete the next *C*, Compassionate, as someone reads 1 Timothy 1:5. Challenge the group to find in that verse a threefold key to keeping a loving relationship with those who oppose you. Share more

deeply from material in "Paul Was Compassionate in His Teachings (1:5)." Pose questions 1 and 2 from the end of the lesson in the *Study Guide*.

7. Complete the fourth *C*, Convinced, as 1 Timothy 1:12–17 is read. Ask, *How did Paul overcome his past to become an effective leader?* Using facts from Acts 7:54—8:3, remind the group of Paul's grievous actions before he was converted. Explain that the doxology in 1:17 is the exuberant praise of a person who had been forgiven much.

Encourage Application

8. Refer to and read aloud from the *Study Guide* the "Case Study" of the single adult leader with a past. Ask the group to choose one or more of these possible actions and explain their choice:
    a. Ignore the complaint of the older member
    b. Counsel the older man, using the example of Paul's past
    c. Replace the single adult leader with someone without a past

9. Close with this question: *Had Paul not allowed God's grace to forgive his past actions, what would the church have lost?*

NOTES

1. Unless otherwise indicated, all Scripture quotations in lessons 1-4 and 8-11 are from the New Revised Standard Version.

MAIN IDEA

Church leaders are to be people of high spiritual qualifications who care faithfully for God's church and serve and represent it well.

QUESTION TO EXPLORE

What should we look for in church leaders?

TEACHING AIM

To lead the class to summarize the instructions about church leaders and list implications for their church's leadership practices

LESSON NINE

Qualities of Worthy Church Leaders

BIBLE COMMENTS

Understanding the Context

Good leadership was hard to find in the time of the early church. Paul and Timothy both knew that. Paul experienced the challenge in his church-planting missionary travels, and Timothy, if not before, experienced it in Ephesus. The issue at Ephesus was the character and theological integrity of the leadership. Notice that in 1 Timothy 1:19–20 Hymenaeus and Alexander "suffered shipwreck in the faith." From 2 Timothy 2:17–18, we learn that Hymenaeus advocated that the resurrection "had already taken place," meaning that the followers of Jesus had experienced resurrection already. How he explained his position is not certain, but he may have believed that the resurrection occurred mystically in baptism, with the dying and rising represented in immersion and raising out of the water. As for Alexander, we have no direct reference to his leadership and teaching. In 2 Timothy 4:14, Paul stated that "Alexander the coppersmith" caused great harm by opposing the message of Paul and his fellow missionaries. He was a negative leader by his opposition to the gospel in whatever form that opposition took.

Leaders come in all sizes and types. One may be dominant in size and verbal volume, able to command a whole room by simply walking into it. He or she attracts others to follow like an exuberant pied piper. Another may be somewhat opposite—quiet, efficient, and inspiring people to express themselves and their abilities for the whole group by her or his less noticeable work behind the scenes. Both types may be good leaders, as well as those who are types that fit in between. Physical characteristics, while they might help in some cases, are not the ultimate explanation for a good leader. This lesson leads us along a path of characteristics that make for good church leadership. A church committed to Christ will seek leadership committed to Christ.

Interpreting the Scriptures

Overseers and Character (3:1–3)

3:1. The saying about aspiring to the "office of bishop" probably came from the secular context about people accepting responsibility in civic life. Paul used the saying to stress the need for leadership to step forward in the church. The word "aspires" is a strong word that goes beyond feelings to actively seeking something. Paul gave prestige to the task by referring to it as "noble," worthy of a person's dedication and best efforts.

The word "bishop" means *overseer,* referring to a general administrative function. It involved responsibilities of providing direction to the whole body of believers as well as performing specific tasks, such as handling finances, welcoming visiting guests, and preaching and teaching.

3:2. Overseers must be "above reproach"; that is, they must keep themselves from moral lapses of judgment or action that might be used to discredit them. The list of attitude and conduct requirements that followed Paul's opening statement was similar to such lists for leaders in Greek society and Jewish synagogue leadership. However, the thrust of this list is distinctively Christian.

The phrase "married only once" is better translated *the husband of one wife,* since the meaning is open to several applications. Does this mean that a person must be married, or married only once, or married to only one person at a time, or that a person whose wife was deceased should not be married again? Or was a celibacy movement in progress by those who believed that sexual relations in marriage made one impure and thus Paul meant, given the widespread promiscuity in that context, that marriage was okay? Because Paul did not elaborate on his meaning, we cannot be dogmatic at this point. He certainly meant that the overseers were to be those who exemplified fidelity in marriage.

Marriage relationship was respected in the Greek culture of Ephesus, but sexual relationships outside of marriage were common. So, again, the emphasis at least was on fidelity to one woman only. Since Paul himself was a person made new by his encounter with Christ, probably bringing a person's previous life before Christ's transforming work into consideration was not a factor. Paul previously being "a blasphemer, a persecutor, and a man of violence" did not keep him from being an apostle (see 1 Timothy 1:12–17).

The overseer was to be "temperate," or *clearheaded,* originally a word used in contrast to an alcohol-muddled head but here applied more broadly. One way of thinking of *clearheaded* is that potential leaders understand the scope of their responsibilities and the directions their leadership and relationships should take. This idea certainly fits the next two words, "sensible" and "respectable," respectively meaning *self-controlled* and *orderly.* Being "hospitable" was necessary in order for Christian traveling missionaries and teachers to be welcomed and supported in the right manner. Having an "apt teacher" in leadership was vital for the ongoing education of the church in the truth of the gospel.

3:3. Drunkenness, violence, and quarrelsomeness marked a person not in control and unable to establish the trust and accessibility necessary for a leader. "A lover of money" was one who placed that love above love for Christ, which is idolatrous. The leader was to be "gentle" with others.

Demonstrated Leadership (3:4–7)

3:4–5. Evidence of a leader's qualifications came from three practical sources. First was home life. How were the prospective leader's family relationships? No family is perfect, but did the potential leader's home context reflect a situation of health and wholesomeness? Children should be held to a standard of obedience. "Respectful in every way" is extremely important here. Some interpreters think "respectful" referred to the conduct of the father, and others think the word applied to the children. Regardless, given that the leader met the other qualifications, respectfulness would be the atmosphere at home. Also, "respectful"— the Greek word also carries the idea of holiness—removed any idea of harshness or abuse, verbally or physically, in order to bring about obedience.

3:6. The second evidence for qualified leadership was that the prospective leader not be "a recent convert." The leader's example in home and church life should be consistent over a reasonable period of time. Such proven maturity kept a person from being "puffed up"; that is, with judgment clouded by pride, a self-importance over others that makes one particularly susceptible to "the devil."

3:7. A third source of evidence was the outside view of the potential leader. Skeptical Jews and pagans naturally viewed the Jesus congregations through the conduct of the leadership, for the leaders would be most visible outside the church. Wrong conduct meant falling into "the snare of the devil," resulting in "disgrace," or into the "reproach" that the bishop must be "above" as cited in 3:2.

Deacons (3:8–10)

3:8–9. "Deacon" is a noble term by virtue of its basic meaning, which is that of *minister* or *servant*. The word referred to one engaged in menial service, such as those designated to be food distributors in Acts 6. Jesus dignified the term by his whole life, because he came "not to be served but to serve, and to give his life a ransom for many" (Mark 10:45). Deacons "likewise" were to possess the character as described for bishops, or overseers. Their conduct must be "serious," not flippant, and their words must be honest, not "double-tongued." They were not to be drunkards or "greedy for money." The "mystery of the faith" that they must live and teach was the work of God's salvation offered to all in Jesus the Christ (see Ephesians 1:3–12).

3:10. Deacons must be "tested." The test to be met was the demonstrated moral conduct as described in 3:8–9. Being "blameless," or having no fault found in them, qualified them to serve as deacons. No person was perfect then as now, but these were the visible guidelines for discerning deacon leadership.

Women (3:11–13)

3:11. The Greek word for *woman* or *wife* is the same word, hence the variation of "wives" (NIV84, KJV) or "women" (NRSV, NASB, NIV) in English translations according to the choice of the translators. Since the word "likewise" follows "women" and since in describing in series the qualities of group leadership in the church, some interpreters conclude that there was an order of women servant leaders in the church. Others see this as referring to the wives of deacons and their conduct. They conclude that Paul would use the term "deaconess" if he meant an order or group. The arguments fall strongly both ways, and this particular text offers no dogmatic solution. The matter of women deacons has to be ultimately settled from additional evidence.

They were to conduct themselves in like manner and demonstrated character as was demanded of the deacons and bishops. The women were not to be "slanderers," or *accusers,* the word thus suggesting gossip that damages someone. They were to be "temperate" in use of alcohol.

3:12–13. Paul returned to the deacons again and brought to bear additional qualities for them that are similar to that of bishops, including the married state and the conduct of their households. Their service done well meant a "good standing" within the community of faith. Good conduct also supported a "boldness in the faith," giving them greater boldness in proclaiming the gospel and also giving them growing confidence about their relationship to God.

Focusing on the Meaning

A quick check on leadership qualities via the internet produces a variety of lists. One site has ten qualities, another has twenty-one qualities, and another has seven. One offers "Leadership Qualities—For Dummies." Reading the various lists offers inspiring qualities but also overwhelms. One of the main elements emerging in the descriptions is the moral quality of the leader.

A list from this lesson's Scripture passage is simpler and more grounded. First is the assumption that a person is a follower of Jesus. A person committed to promoting self or a personal agenda is contrary to serving Jesus. Second is a desire to serve. Service implies work, and the work is work for Christ and in behalf of the well being of the church. Third, one is to live out the ethical teachings of Jesus, both in the church and in the world.

As to the role of servants, the church should not think of church leaders in terms of servitude, as in that the leaders should conform to personal wishes and agendas. On the other hand, leadership should not be thought of as holding an office as we tend to do in our present culture. Rather, as is obvious from the context, being a bishop is a function of service, and being a deacon is a function of service. Think of Jesus' title, the "Christ," meaning that he is King. What kind of King was (is) he? Did he expect to be served or recognized for being an office-bearer? His life and the cross answer that question.

As followers of Jesus we are all servants, or ministers. We are the body of Christ, and each part of the body has its function (see 1 Corinthians 12:12–21). Each part functions for the health of the whole body, the church. Also, leaders are not the head of the body; rather, Jesus is (Eph. 1:22–23). Jesus continues to serve through the church. Being led by and in Jesus makes good leaders.

TEACHING PLANS

Teaching Plan—Varied Learning Activities

Connect with Life

1. Consider conducting an interview with one of your staff ministers or a deacon (either in person or via video or audio recording). Arrange early in the week, and explain that the interview should take about fifteen minutes at the beginning of the study hour. Give these questions ahead so your guest's answers can be thoughtful and concise.
   - Some ministers and deacons feel called of God to their task, while others see their role as more of a profession than a calling. Can you tell us how you decided to take on this ministering role?
   - Ministry, whether professional or volunteer, requires a unique set of abilities and spiritual gifts. Which parts of your ministry do you feel you do best? Which are more difficult for you?
   - What kind of education is useful for a person in your profession or calling?

- Often there is some tension in balancing the roles of family life, personal health, and ministry. How have you learned to prioritize those responsibilities?
- Can you suggest some ways we in this study group can partner with you to help in your ministry?

2. Consider these suggestions for conducting the interview:
   - Let the group know ahead of time so they can help you host the occasion.
   - Introduce the guest (even if he or she is well known to the group), and thank the person for the person's work.
   - Make every question positive, and receive every answer in a non-critical way.
   - Inquire ahead about whether the guest is willing to take additional questions from the class.
   - Be genuine in thanks and praise when the interview is finished.

Guide Bible Study

3. Invite the group to act as a search committee seeking new leaders for your church. Form two teams to create job descriptions based on 1 Timothy 3. (If attendance is small, one or two people can form a team. In larger classes, several teams may work on the same assignment.) Allow five minutes for teams to search their assigned verses and list the qualifications God has given for that job.

   Team One: Overseer and Pastor Job Description (1 Timothy 3:1–7)
   Team Two: Deacon Job Description (1 Timothy 3:8–12)

4. Ask a spokesperson from each group to present the findings of the group as a second person lists the qualifications on the board.

5. Follow team reports with these questions for open discussion:
   - Which qualifications are mentioned in both lists?
   - How important is the family to a leader's effectiveness? (Add enrichment from the *Study Guide* section, "Leadership in the Church Is a Worthy Task (3:10)," and the small article, "Family and Leadership.")

- Which qualifications speak directly to the character and integrity of a leader? (Add from the section, "Leadership in the Church Requires Worthy Character (3:2–12).")
- What special cautions are given to women?

6. Read 1 Timothy 3:13 and point out two rewards that come to those who faithfully fulfill their tasks in ministry. Refer to the section in the *Study Guide* under the heading, "Leadership in the Church Is Rewarded with Worthy Assurances (3:13)."

Encourage Application

7. Give a blank thank-you note and envelope to each person. Suggest that they take them home and write a note of encouragement to one of the ministers or deacons of your congregation.

8. Invite group members to sign up for a prayer chain supporting the church ministry staff and leaders. Secure a volunteer to take names and e-mail addresses, and to maintain the list so that special needs can be communicated quickly for prayer. Alert the church staff that you have a group standing ready to pray for them at any time.

Teaching Plan—Lecture and Questions

Connect with Life

1. Lead the class to help you draw a profile of your church to serve as a backdrop for today's study of church leaders. Give each attendee the following questions (a copy of the questions is available in "Teaching Resource Items" for this study at www.baptistwaypress.org):
   (1) Where does our church meet: in a traditional building, a borrowed building, a rented storefront, a home, on multiple campuses, or other?
   (2) How many ordained ministers currently serve on our staff?
   (3) Are our deacons ordained or elected?
   (4) Do we ordain women as deacons or ministers?

(5) How are decisions and plans made in our church: by staff, elders, deacons, committees, the congregation as a whole, or another way?

(6) What are the strengths of our church: evangelism, worship, ministry to needy, church planting, other?

(7) What do you personally like best about our church?

2. Refer to and read the Main Idea and Study Aim for this lesson from the *Study Guide*.

Guide Bible Study

3. Define the two leadership positions, overseers and deacons, addressed in 1 Timothy 3:1–13. Use material in the *Study Guide* section, "Leadership in the Church Is Rewarded with Worthy Assurances (3:13)." On the board write:

Overseers = Elders and Pastors
Deacons = Servant Leaders

4. Make a two-column chart with the title, "Overseers." Label column 1, "Family Life," and column 2, "Personal Character." Ask the group to help you make a running list of the qualifications mentioned in 1 Timothy 3:1–7.
   • Under "Family Life," help them discover the characteristics that apply (see 3:2, 4–5).
   • Under "Personal Character," help them list the characteristics that apply (see 3:2–3, 6–7).

5. Create a second chart with the title, "Deacons." Use the same two subtitles, and again ask members to help you find the qualifications in 1 Timothy 3:8–12.
   • Under "Personal Character," lead the class to identify the characteristics that apply (see 3:8–10).
   • Under "Family Life," lead the class to identify the characteristics that apply (see 3:11–12).

6. Conclude with 1 Timothy 3:13, and emphasize that church leaders who serve well will grow spiritually and are deserving of our respect and gratitude.

Encourage Application

7. Select questions for further discussion from those near the end of the lesson in the *Study Guide*. Also consider these:
   - Does our church have added expectations of our pastor and deacons? Are our expectations in keeping with the lists just studied?
   - Do these lists form a life model that other members should try to emulate?

8. Pose the case study from the small article, "Tired and Burned Out," in the *Study Guide*.

9. Invite members to become secret prayer partners to one minister and one deacon in your church family during the remainder of this six-week study of 1 and 2 Timothy.

FOCAL TEXT
1 Timothy 4

BACKGROUND
1 Timothy 4

MAIN IDEA
Paul instructed Timothy to train himself for godliness in order to ensure his own spiritual welfare and also to be prepared to lead others to walk in that way themselves.

QUESTION TO EXPLORE
In what ways do you intentionally seek to train yourself for godliness?

TEACHING AIM
To lead adults to identify specific ways for training themselves for godliness and decide on at least one they will put into practice

LESSON TEN
Train for Godliness

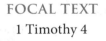

BIBLE COMMENTS

Understanding the Context

Everyone has a view, a belief system, and/or an interpretation of life by which she or he lives. The ever-present ministry of the church is to help people to find themselves in relation to the gospel of Jesus Christ. An additional challenge to the church is to equip Christians, through sound teaching and faithful Christian living, to answer wrong views that are in the culture all around us.

The opponents Timothy encountered at Ephesus had distinct views out of which they thought and acted. Represented in their views were two streams of thought. First was a Jewish stream that included emphasis on certain laws and engagement in disputes over the law, genealogies, and certain fables. Second was a developing Gnostic stream, a philosophy that had at its base a belief that the material, all things of matter including the human body, was evil. Only the spirit was good. So they advocated certain ascetic practices such as rejecting marriage with its sexual relations and abstaining from certain foods. Hence, the physical body does not participate in salvation. To hold this view ultimately meant one had to deny the incarnation and the bodily resurrection of Jesus. These false teachers, out of their flawed and ill-defined belief systems, threatened sound Christian teaching, sowed discord, and engaged in morally deficient lifestyles.

Timothy's cultural situation was much like ours in terms of its challenges. What was he, and what are we, to do? Paul advised Timothy to engage in godly training for himself and for the church. What did being godly involve? Was it a suppression of one's physical self in order to accept a spiritual status? How were Timothy and the church to train for godly living?

Interpreting the Scriptures

First, Define Objectively the Evil That Counters Godly Living (4:1)

Jesus warned that false leaders would appear and even do mighty works in an attempt to convince people to follow them (Mark 13:22). Not surprising here, then, that the Spirit continued to warn of the danger. The "deceitful spirits" and "demons" were the source of the danger. "Deceitful spirits" referenced the influence of the evil one, Satan, behind errant teachings. Evil takes demonic shape in people and institutions. A person who steals is a person used by the demonic. An institution that oppresses people, whether political, economic, or social institutions, is used by the demonic. Behind every conflict that fights the good is a demonic influence. The demonic, or Satan, however, has no power over us except what we give it individually and collectively. Sound teaching and godly living are the means of deliverance against the subtle influences of the demonic that makes its way into the culture around us and possibly into the church. Evidently, evil's influence led some at Ephesus to "renounce the faith."

The word "times," in "later times," translates the Greek word *kairos*, which refers to a season of time. The other Greek word for time, *chronos*, refers to chronological time. A season of time—*kairos*—is indefinite according to chronology, and so one can be in a season of time for a long time. That does not, however, remove the urgency in this context. Jesus is the beginning and the end (Revelation 1:17–18; 22:13), and so the end of all things is with him just as sure as he is our beginning. In this sense we always live in the end times as eternity always impinges on the present. We move through this un-chronological season of time toward the consummation of all things, toward the return of Jesus the Christ.

Second, Recognize the Motivation and Practice of Evil Against Godly Living (4:2–3)

4:2. The source of the deceptive influence was through "liars." Their teaching was false. They came to their positions through "seared" consciences. Their sensitivity to truth was inoperative as a result of their burned-over ability to accept moral guidance. They were hypocrites in that they convinced themselves to believe that which was not true.

Hence, they did not merely *pretend* that the lie was true. Rather they deceived themselves into *believing* the lie was true. Their seared consciences prevented them from allowing the truth to expose their error so they could live by the truth.

4:3. They forbade "marriage," believing sexual relations to be evil even in marriage. They fell into legalism, judging godliness by a set of rules such as abstaining from certain foods. The motivation behind this regimen was the problem, however. They viewed the body as evil, composed of material substance that imprisoned the spiritual. They believed that to escape as much evil as possible a person must refrain from marriage and certain foods. Such ideas ultimately denied the humanity of Christ and his total salvation that overcomes evil's fragmentation and makes his followers into whole people. The lie led to bad conclusions and bad practices.

Third, Know the Truth That Answers the Evil (4:4–5)

The truth is that God created the physical, and God creates only good. To assure that the physical or material is good for us, Paul stressed that the creation be received with "thanksgiving." A person who followed this right teaching understood that the good was from God and was to be appropriated or experienced in ways consistent with God's goodness.

"Sanctified" means to remove from the status of the profane. Since God created the material, such as food, it comes to us "sanctified." We sanctify it to ourselves by recognizing it as God's gift and accepting it, consequently, in thanksgiving.

Such a common thing as a blessing at meals prepares us with thanksgiving to receive what God provides. In a sense, receiving with thanksgiving sanctifies the food to us.

Fourth, Teach and Live the Truth for Godly Living (4:6–7)

"Put these instructions before" carries the idea of putting the instructions *under* them, suggesting foundational teaching. Paul took a positive approach as to what Timothy was to do. He was to teach that which was right. Timothy would have the ability to do so since he would be "nourished" by "faith" and "sound teaching." He was to distance himself from

"profane myths"—those claims that were unholy—and "old wives' tales."
In the philosophical argumentation of the day, a debater might attack
sarcastically an opponent's views as "old wives' tales," which meant they
had no basis in truth. Timothy's energy was best used in training "in
godliness."

Fifth, Put Forth the Energy for Training in Godly Living (4:8–13)

4:8–10. Two athletic analogies occur: "physical training" (4:8) and "toil
and struggle" (4:10), both in the sense of running a race. The analogies
pictured godly living in terms of athletic competition. In contrast to the
"profane myths and old wives' tales" and the exertion that both of those
called for in order for people to follow them, Timothy was to give his
energies to training in godliness. Growth in the knowledge and understanding of God as revealed in Jesus is the far better exertion, for it is
exertion toward the "living God." Both "promise" (4:8) and "hope" (4:10)
are the prizes at the conclusion of the race, but Timothy had begun to
experience both already through the discipline of training in godliness.

4:11–13. The words of Paul suggest that the church tensions threatened
to overwhelm Timothy. "Must insist" is a command, much as a military command. Timothy's own conduct "in love, in faith, in purity," all
positive actions, were foundational for him to authenticate his public
leadership. Thus as Timothy read Scripture, exhorted the people to act
on the gospel, and taught them the way of godly living, he would be
viewed as a person who practiced what he proclaimed.

Sixth, Recognize Your Giftedness For Training in Godly Living (4:14–16)

Timothy's giftedness meant he had the endowments necessary to do
the work of his calling. The Spirit worked through "prophecy" in those
around him by which they determined the gift in Timothy for his calling (and especially so Paul, see 2 Timothy 1:6–7). "The laying on of
hands" confirmed Timothy's calling on the part of the church through
the action of the "elders." Although not identified, the "elders" probably
were a group of leaders who worked with Paul.

By Timothy's faithfulness, both Timothy and his hearers would be saved. To "save" is in the future tense. Many are familiar with the security of having been saved once for all, and that is true, but we also are *being* saved, and we *will be* saved. Salvation comes to its fulfillment in the future. Faithful leadership in the present salvation brings Christ-like growth toward the future salvation.

Timothy and his hearers were to practice godly living and thus to grow together in godly living. Jesus the Christ has gifted his church for training in godly living and for living out the training in the midst of challenging cultural beliefs.

Focusing on the Meaning

If we are to engage in training for godly living, we must be astute enough to recognize that which is not godly. Defining what is not godly is important. It becomes vague in our minds if we do not. Also, defining it helps us to keep the evil separate from the good. We do not fixate on the evil, however, but rather we bring the truth corresponding to the evil to bear against the evil. All evil is a perversion of the good. Good exists first, and evil attempts to pervert the good.

In recognizing evil and responding to it, we must treat more than the symptoms. A false foundation underlies the evil. God's truth as expressed in his revelation, particularly and ultimately in Jesus our Lord, is so important to freeing one from a "seared" conscience, which disrupts life and robs one of real life. But more is required than words, as important as words are. The practice must be there. One can hold intellectual propositions about matters, know about the correct teaching, but never *really* know them unless they are one's lifestyle. Some have said that it takes twenty-one days to form a new habit, but that time frame evidently is simply arbitrary. Time depends on the person and the habit. However, daily practice moves the transition along rapidly, and training in godliness is a daily matter. Teaching and practicing what is taught makes an authentic teacher.

Training in godliness can seem a bit self-righteous. Such training also can become legalistic. Legalists usually choose their rules of right behavior, leaving off those that are difficult for them to keep. Then it is easier to condemn those who do not meet the list. However, we have no basis for self-righteousness or legalism. Training in godliness is a response to God's grace and love. Neither, however, are we to back off from, in Christ's love, opposing the wrong. Paul's instruction to Timothy was to train in the positive message of godly living, which offers the opportunity to be affirming rather than condemning.

TEACHING PLANS

Teaching Plan—Varied Learning Activities

Connect with Life

1. Begin with this show-of-hands survey:
   (1) How many of you belong to a fitness club or an exercise group?
   (2) How many exercise on your own and try to "eat healthy"?
   (3) Which of you feels you are in better shape physically today than you were three years ago?
2. Point out that this lesson has to do with our fitness plan but not so much with our physical conditioning. Refer to and read the Quick Read and Question to Explore at the beginning of this lesson in the *Study Guide.*

Guide Bible Study

3. Hand out copies of "Timothy's Fitness Plan." (A copy is available in "Teaching Resource Items" for this study at www.baptistwaypress.org.) Provide pens or pencils. Explain that the group will walk through the form and read the Bible verses together. Encourage members to suggest practical ways to plan, perform, and achieve each section. (See step 4 for questions and suggestions that will facilitate this activity.)

Timothy's Fitness Plan
A Way to Train for Godliness (1 Timothy 4:1–16)

I. Some things to *resist* if you would be spiritually fit (1 Tim. 4:1–6)

- Avoiding spiritual laziness, and staying alert to truth (4:1)

  _____

  _____

- Things that are detrimental to my training for godliness (4:2–3)

  _____

  _____

- A more wholesome attitude toward life (4:4–6)

  _____

  _____

II. Some things to include if you would gain *strength* spiritually (1 Tim. 4:7–11)

- Setting priorities for my time and my life (4:8)

  _____

  _____

- Sorting out biblical truth from false teachings (4:7, 9–11)

  _____

  _____

III. Setting an *example* of godliness for others (1 Tim. 4:12–16)

- Five areas in which to set an example (4:12)

  _____

  _____

- The values of public/corporate worship (4:13)

  _____

  _____

> • Developing the spiritual gift(s) you have been given
> (4:14)
>
> _____
>
> _____
>
> • Sticking with the program (4:15–16)
>
> _____
>
> _____

4. Use questions like these to help the group think more deeply about "Timothy's Fitness Plan":
   - *Resist* (1 Tim. 4:1–6): What tempts Christians to become lazy "couch potatoes" and neglect spiritual disciplines? Can you identify religious groups that impose rules that are not found in the New Testament? What characterizes preaching that compromises Bible truths? When it comes to diet, is there a difference between what God created and things people have developed? What must we do if we are to better know and live by Bible truths?
   - *Strength* (1 Tim. 4:7–11): Is it realistic to suggest that a Christian should spend as much time in spiritual training as he or she does in physical conditioning? What activities take time that we could dedicate to Bible study, prayer, and reading or experiencing wholesome Christian teaching? Is Jesus automatically the Savior of all people or only of those who choose to accept and believe in him? (Refer to the small article, "The Savior of All People," in the *Study Guide.*)
   - *Example* (1 Tim. 4:12–16): To whom should you be an example of the Christian life? What brief definition would you suggest for each of these five areas: speech, life, love, faith, and purity? Why are people often undisciplined about church participation? What is your spiritual gift, and how are you developing and using it? How can a believer have accountability in matters of behavior and witness?

Encourage Application

5. Challenge the group to turn their copy of "Timothy's Fitness Plan" over and use the back to keep a journal for one week. Give these instructions:

   (1) List in the left column the five areas in which we are to set an example: speech, life, love, faith, and purity.

   (2) In the right column, journal ways in which you are able to set an example in word, action, and attitude this week.

   (3) Suggest that those who wish to may find an accountability partner within the class, exchange phone or email information, and encourage each other during the week.

Teaching Plan—Lecture and Questions

Connect with Life

1. Refer to and tell the story of Coach Berry at the beginning of this lesson in the *Study Guide*. On the board write two words from the story: "Training" and "Witness." Read the Main Idea of the lesson, noting that these two key words are prominent in today's study.

2. Print three questions on paper or poster board and post them on the focal wall:
   - Does this make me weaker as a Christian?
   - Could this help me become a stronger Christian?
   - Will this help me point people to Christ?

   Note that these are key questions if we are to accept today's challenge to "Train for Godliness."

Guide Bible Study

3. Call on someone to read 1 Timothy 4:1–6 as the group listens for things to resist or avoid, things which make us weaker Christians. Help them find ideas like these: falling away from faithfulness;

following deceiving leaders and ideas; substituting non-biblical rules for true godliness; imposing legalistic rules on other people.

Follow with these questions and additional ideas from the *Study Guide* section, "Resistance Training (4:1–6)."

- Are we to be surprised or discouraged when people leave the faith?
- What makes these deceiving leaders and ideas so attractive to weaker Christians?
- Which is easier: to keep rules or to develop disciplines that make us stronger Christians?
- How can we warn our friends about these things?

4. Invite a volunteer to read 1 Timothy 4:7–11 as the class listens for the comparison between physical fitness training and training for godliness. Note that both have value, but one is not to exclude the other.

   Pose this question for debate: *Should a Christian spend more time and effort in spiritual disciplines such as Bible study, prayer, and service, than he or she spends in physical fitness routines and pastimes?* Follow with, *How do we set priorities that help us find balance in these two areas?*

5. As someone reads 1 Timothy 4:12–16, ask members to choose and note which verse of those five speaks most pointedly to them. Invite brief sharing of choices and reasons. Lead the group to help you summarize each verse in a concise sentence. Consider these examples:
   - Verse 12. Set an example in all areas of life.
   - Verse 13. Be faithful in worship and Bible study.
   - Verse 14. Develop your God-given abilities.
   - Verse 15. Be fully accountable and transparent.
   - Verse 16. Be vigilant about your witness, your influence on others.

Offer additional insights from the *Study Guide* section, "Core Training (4:12–16)."

Encourage Application

6. Refer to the three questions posted on the focal wall (see step 2). Suggest that each person jot them down in his or her Bible (perhaps

near 1 Timothy 4 or on a flyleaf page of his or her Bible) or in the *Study Guide* for future accountability.

7. Give out sheets from a small sticky pad and encourage everyone to write down one or more names of people they should point to Christ by the example of their lives. They might place these by the three questions as a prayer reminder that they are providing a positive or negative example to them every day.

FOCAL TEXT
1 Timothy 6:3–19

BACKGROUND
1 Timothy 6

MAIN IDEA

Christians must emphasize godliness rather than seeking material wealth and must use the wealth they have for God's purposes.

QUESTION TO EXPLORE

Is our attitude toward and use of our money truly Christlike?

TEACHING AIM

To lead the class to evaluate their attitude toward and use of money in light of this lesson's teachings about material wealth

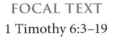

LESSON ELEVEN
God or Money?

BIBLE COMMENTS

Understanding the Context

Our culture has perhaps three negative relationships to money: greed for money, unwise use of money, and no or insufficient money. First, there is the desire for money for money's value and power. Greed drives the desire, and such desire always brings destructiveness to someone. Second, there is the unwise use of money that drives people to overextend their capacity, which creates hardship. Third, many people have little or no money. Sometimes a few dollars cannot be found to purchase a small part for the truck so that a person can go to a job that pays minimal support. Or, a catastrophic illness or other money-draining events deplete people of savings and income. The use of or lack of wealth can become a very difficult problem.

Of course, wealth is more than money. What is true wealth, and how does money function within true wealth? This lesson moves us to consider certain instructions that aid in answering these questions. Among other problems, the church at Ephesus faced a challenge concerning money. Timothy, left in charge of the congregation by Paul after he and Paul worked together at Ephesus, had to deal with the issue. The emphasis is on a godly relationship to wealth. Money is a small but important part of that wealth, and we are to use it wisely in relationship to God and others. If we do, we will become part of the solution to the unhealthy relationships to money.

Remember that one temptation of Jesus after his baptism was to turn stones into bread (see Matthew 4:3–4). Among other aspects of this temptation was for Jesus to rule, bring in his kingdom, by the manipulation of economic power. Jesus' response was that what God says is more important than even having needed bread to sustain life. Bread is a necessity for life, but real life is first and foremost living by God's will and purpose, which includes the use of wealth.

Interpreting the Scriptures

Jesus or a Desire for Money? (6:3–5)

6:3. The expression "whoever teaches otherwise" indicates that wrong teaching was Paul's target. What is right teaching? Jesus Christ is at the center, and what the church teaches should reflect him. Words, doctrines, interpretations are important in the responsibilities of the teacher and the church, but the gospel is a Person. Does anything we teach contrast with the Jesus we meet in the apostolic witness of the New Testament along with the witness of the Holy Spirit in our own lives? If so, we either have the wrong view of Jesus or we have the wrong view contained in what we teach. A television personality who promises healing if someone buys his anointed prayer cloth so that he can pad his own pocket perverts the gospel. He denies who Jesus is and was, what he taught, and above all what the cross is about as well. The teaching that is "in accordance with godliness" is in accordance with our Lord, including our motivation for and use of money.

6:4. Paul mounted a withering attack on those who did not teach in accordance with godliness. They were "conceited, understanding nothing." Conceited means "puffed up," full of pride. Such people listened to themselves and not to sound teaching founded in Jesus. They understood "nothing" since their pride insulated them from the truth.

People so described were lightning rods for controversy. They desired to win disputes in order to advance their agendas. "Morbid craving" is like one who has a sickness and continues to hold on to it. The results from this behavior to a church or a community are destructive, resulting in "envy, dissension, slander," and "base suspicions." Paul and Timothy knew these dangers.

6:5. Constant "wrangling" arose out of "depraved" minds "bereft of the truth." The word "mind" involved the intellect, the emotion, and the will of a person; in short, "mind" referred to the whole person. The "depraved" minds, empty as they were of the ability to discern the truth, were incapable of sound moral judgment. They purposed to earn profit, "gain," by their teaching. Exactly how, whether to profit by charging for their teachings or collecting offerings from a gullible public, is uncertain.

Whatever the case, they placed monetary gain over teaching the truth. The truth of Jesus is to occupy first place, not money.

What Is the Greatest Gain? (6:6–10)

6:6. In direct contrast to seeking monetary gain is to seek to gain in "godliness" and "contentment." Neither godliness nor contentment comes solely by one's own power. How are we to think of "godliness"? Reflecting back to 1 Timothy 6:3, we see that Jesus is the measure of godliness because he is "God . . . with us" (Matt. 1:23). We are to seek to be like Jesus. In his Letter to the Philippians, Paul described contentment in reference to his own experience. There he basically said that circumstances do not determine the level of one's contentment (Philippians 4:11–13). He was okay in whatever circumstances.

Riches do not determine contentment. Contentment indicates a frame of mind that views one's life as one of sufficiency, whatever the circumstances. Jesus' sovereignty, love, and walk with us are sufficient, including how we are to use our wealth.

6:7–9. Paul showed that it makes sense to put God first. People do not bring with them anything at birth, and neither do they take anything with them on leaving this life. "Food and clothing," of course, are necessary to sustain life while we are of this life. The point is that if people become focused on riches, seeking first that which is not really important to eternal life, they fall into "temptation." Submission to temptation leaves people "trapped" into desires that lead to "ruin and destruction." The destruction is the loss of that which cannot be reclaimed. To give oneself to wealth is to give oneself to that which does not save life.

6:10. It is the "love" of money that is "a root of all kinds of evil." The statement must be taken in context, for there are other devotions, or loves, that lead people to evil. The love of power, for example, is a terrible root of evil. Paul especially had in mind the false teachers about whom he warned Timothy. Love of money does lead to all kinds of evil. Striving for wealth causes people to go astray from the "faith." "Faith" in this context refers to the doctrines, or sound teachings, of Christianity. Nevertheless, they did this to themselves. Because of their own "eagerness to be rich," they "wandered away from the faith and pierced themselves with many pains."

The Way to the Greatest Gain (6:11–19)

6:11. Obviously, we want to avoid piercing ourselves with "many pains." But what do we put in the place of the love for and pursuit of wealth? We "pursue righteousness, godliness, faith, love, endurance, gentleness." All of these attributes are about relationships, first to God and then to others. So, relationships are where true wealth resides, beginning with relationship to God.

6:12. Paul instructed Timothy that Timothy needed to "fight the good fight of faith" for at least two reasons. First he was in God's service, a call to which Timothy had personally responded. Second, Timothy had publicly acknowledged his commitment in the "presence of many witnesses," who would expect him to stand against the false teachers. To "take hold of eternal life" meant to take hold of that which was of eternal investment, an eternity that begins in the present with the blessings of relationship to Jesus.

6:13–16. Paul reminded Timothy of the great ministry to which God had called him. God's "presence" and the courageous example of Jesus before Pilate were sound motivations to keep to his ministry. To discharge ministry without "spot" or "blame" was to give no cause for criticism to come upon his ministry. While the present challenges might be difficult, everything moved toward the goal of the return of Jesus.

God is the "King," not selfish teachers or the power of money. While God could not be seen by Timothy or anyone, there was no doubt about God's dominion. God is immortal; riches are not. That God dwells in "unapproachable light" meant that God's holiness, his righteousness, is so great that human beings' impurity keeps them from seeing God. The luster of riches pales in the light of God's greatness.

6:17–19. Paul knew that some people had money. His message to them was straightforward. They were not to be "haughty," that is, to think of themselves in exalted terms. They were to set "their hopes . . . on God who richly provides," not on riches that do not really provide. They were to be "rich in good works," hence using their riches to bring good to others. To do so made them richer, because people, not money, have eternal futures. When Paul mentioned "storing up," he might have had in mind Jesus' teaching to "store up for yourselves treasures in heaven" (Matt. 6:20). People, not things, go to heaven, and thus investing in people is an eternal investment. So, "those who in the present age are rich" were to "take hold of the life that really is life." This "life" is the eternal life given to us out of the riches of God through the sacrificial service of Jesus.

Focusing on the Meaning

One of the struggles for Timothy was to overcome those who wanted to direct what little wealth the church had toward themselves. According to Paul's instructions, Timothy was to combat the negative influence of money through emphasizing the sovereignty of God, centering his teaching and his and others' commitments on the person of Jesus, living lives consistent with following Jesus, and investing wealth in others as an eternal investment. Consequently, the real wealth is in relationship to God through Jesus and in relationship to others. Emphasizing those relationships is the basis for developing a healthy and wise use of wealth.

Paul's concern was for the church, and the first place to perceive of the right use of money is in reference to the church. A primary way of ordering the use of wealth is to give to and through the church. A tithe as the minimum standard for giving has its roots in biblical practice. Christians often share testimonies that putting the tithe first helped them to a healthy order for the rest of their resources, since both in concept and practice tithing was an act of putting God first.

Of course, Jesus calls us to be one-hundred-percent givers, seeking to bring all of our time, talent, and resources under his lordship. One of the practices in which we can engage is to take inventory of where our money is going. We can look at each bill paid and ask ourselves about how this particular payment relates to God, the teachings of Jesus, our families, and others. How is each a ministry or how may each be directed toward ministry? Paying the mechanic for repair to one's car, for example, enables the mechanic to provide shelter, food, and clothing for his family. Could not my attitude, a prayer for the mechanic and his family and workers, and a word of witness enrich the money paid as ministry? What about the other outgoing monies? How could they be ministries in the name of Jesus?

TEACHING PLANS

Teaching Plan—Varied Learning Activities

Connect with Life

1. Begin by telling this true story. (The name and some details have been changed.)

> Kathleen was a single mother, struggling to stretch her paycheck through the month, raising a four-year-old daughter. A broken marriage had left her with large debts, not of her making. She came to work full time as a secretary at the church office, but she also took on part-time positions as a childcare worker and hostess after hours. Her faith shone through, and she tithed of all her incomes regularly. She gave generously of her time, her many talents, and her finances.
>
> As time went on, Kathleen was offered better positions in the secular world, and her skills and integrity paid off in promotions and raises. Always she gave her tithe and much more, while continuing a modest lifestyle. Hers was an amazing *rags to riches* story as she rose from meager pay to a good salary, and later to ownership in a thriving company. One would think that Kathleen and her (now larger) family would move up to a more lavish lifestyle and home, but that did not happen. She chose to live in a modest neighborhood and give more generously to her church and other kingdom causes. Kathleen is one who did not shape

her money around herself but shaped her money around God's good news, as the *Study Guide* states.

2. Give each person (or couple) a clear plastic bag on which you have placed this label: "God's Stuff." Invite them to put their wallets, credit cards, pocket change, and checkbooks in the bag. Follow by referring to and reading the Quick Read and Study Aim in the lesson in the *Study Guide*.

Guide Bible Study

3. Remind the group that 1 Timothy was written to warn against false teachings in the church. (See "Shaping our Wealth Around False Doctrine" in the *Study Guide*.) Read 1 Timothy 6:3–5 as the group listens for a false doctrine about money (see 1 Tim. 6:5).

4. Write on the board, "Getting Money (1 Tim. 6:6–10)." Instruct the group to listen to the verses and formulate a Christian plan for getting money. After they share thoughts, summarize with these points.
   • Godliness is basic, and wealth is secondary.
   • Contentment requires only that basic needs be met.
   • Greed is a trap that makes us vulnerable to temptations.

5. Add to the board, "Spending Money (1 Tim. 6:11–16)." As these verses are read, ask the group to listen for the six things to pursue before pursuing material possessions (6:11). List on the board: *righteousness, godliness, faith, love, endurance,* and *gentleness*. Give each person a small sheet of paper, and ask them to jot down private thoughts about their attitudes about money. Use these questions to guide their thoughts:
   (1) Is my first priority in life to grow in godliness and righteousness?
   (2) Do my attitudes about spending money help or hinder my being generous?
   (3) Do my checkbooks and credit card statements witness to my faith?
   (4) Is there some change I should make regarding how I spend my money?

(A copy of these questions is available in "Teaching Resource Items" for this study at www.baptistwaypress.org.)

6. Add to the board, "Giving Money (1 Tim. 6:17–19)." Ask members to listen for the *do nots* and *dos* in these verses. List their responses. Consider these examples:
   - *Do not*: be arrogant, trust in wealth for security, take credit for success.
   - *Do*: many good works, share willingly, keep eternal reward in view.

Encourage Application

7. Refer to the next-to-last paragraph under the heading "How We Shape Our Wealth Around Sound Doctrine" in the *Study Guide*. Enlist someone to read the paragraph, which begins with the words, "Paul told Timothy. . . ." Invite comments about how Christians should respond.

8. Close by referring to and reading the small article, "A Theology of Wealth," in the *Study Guide*. Remind learners that everything in their plastic bags is "God's Stuff" and how we make and spend it should be God's to decide.

Teaching Plan—Lecture and Questions

Connect with Life

1. Begin by referring to and telling the funny story about the misprint in the new Bible at the beginning of this lesson in the *Study Guide*. Follow by referring to and reading the Study Aim and Question to Explore in the *Study Guide*.

2. Lead members to take a short survey about their spending habits. (This can be written or open.)
   (1) How often do you and your family members eat out?
   (2) Do you purchase from "junk food" vending machines?

(3) What is your rule of thumb when it comes to buying new clothes?

(4) Which of the newest electronic items will probably be your next purchase?

3. Post this quote from near the end of this lesson in the *Study Guide*: "The richest 20 percent of the population of the world consumes 90 percent of the goods produced while the poorest 20 percent consume 1 percent." Warn the group that Paul's writings to Timothy in this lesson will, and probably should, make us ask questions about our money and how we use it.

Guide Bible Study

4. Remind the group that Paul wrote this letter to Timothy to combat false teachings, and that applies also to teachings about money. Read 1 Timothy 6:3–5, emphasizing the last phrase of verse 5. Follow with these discussion questions:
   - Can you think of anyone who uses religion to get wealthy? (Point out that, while we do not own mansions and luxury cars, often we do hope that when we please God he will reward us with financial blessings.)
   - Is it wrong for us to expect blessings in return for our devotion to God?
   - Did Jesus have material things in mind when he spoke the words in Matthew 6:33? (Jesus taught and modeled a simple lifestyle, and this verse follows his teachings on piety and generosity.)
   - Why do you think Jesus asked the rich man in Mark 10:21–22 to sell out and become a disciple? (Wealth can be a distraction when a person commits to serious discipleship.)

5. Read 1 Timothy 6:6–10 as the group listens for a definition of contentment. Invite comments. Respond to their views, and emphasize verses 7–8. Ask, *How can a simplified lifestyle make it easier to seek holiness and godliness? On the other hand, how can pursuit of wealth make us vulnerable to temptations?*

6. Read 1 Timothy 6:11–16 as the group listens for what we are to *flee,* and what we are to "pursue." Ask, *In our media-driven world, how does a Christian "flee" the temptation to buy, buy, buy?*

Enlist a volunteer to do an internet search for a profile of Mother Teresa and to report on it. After the report, help the group recall her lifestyle and ministry in Calcutta. Pose these questions for discussion:

- On a scale of *1* to *10,* 1 being pursuit of holiness and godliness, and *10* being living selfishly, where do you think she would figure in? Where would you place Jesus?
- Is it necessary to be poor in order to be holy and godly?
- Can a person be wealthy and still keep a strong hold on the faith? How?

7. Read verses 17–19 as the group looks for positive uses of our wealth. List their findings on the board.

Encourage Application

8. Close by referring to and sharing the small article, "Things to Do about Wealth," in the *Study Guide.*

FOCAL TEXT
2 Timothy 1:6–14; 2:1–15

BACKGROUND
2 Timothy 1—2

MAIN IDEA
Paul called Timothy to focus again on serving Christ and to keep on being faithful.

QUESTION TO EXPLORE
What encouragement do you need today to wake up and get going again in serving Christ?

TEACHING AIM
To lead participants to decide to awaken again to serving Christ and to keep on being faithful

LESSON TWELVE
Wake Up and Keep Going

BIBLE COMMENTS

Understanding the Context

Second Timothy is one of the letters that are called "The Pastoral Epistles (Letters)." Along with First Timothy and Titus, these were the letters Paul wrote to his young associates and pastors. Timothy was the pastor at Ephesus, while Titus was the pastor in Crete. It is sometimes suggested that they might have been overseers of several churches.

Second Timothy is the last of Paul's letters that we have. One must note what this says and what it is not saying. It is not saying that Second Timothy was the last letter Paul ever wrote. Paul was a prolific writer, and Paul could very well have written one or more letters after Second Timothy. But if he did, we don't have them. We are also not suggesting that Paul wrote this letter from his deathbed. Paul urged Timothy to endeavor to come to see him "before winter" (2 Timothy 4:21).[1] He also asked Timothy to bring with him John Mark, the cloak Paul had left with Carpus at Troas, and Paul's scrolls (see 2 Tim. 4:11–13). All of these meant that he was expecting to live to see the following winter.

Paul addressed Timothy affectionately as "my dear son" (1:2). In First Timothy, Paul had addressed Timothy as "my true son in the faith" (1 Timothy 1:2). Timothy was Paul's son-in-the-Lord, not because Paul was the one who had led him to the Lord but because Paul was the one who had discipled him. When Paul first met Timothy at Lystra, Timothy was already a believer who was well spoken of by the brethren in Lystra and Iconium (see Acts 16:1–2).

In 2 Timothy, Paul, who believed that the time of his departure from this earth was near (2 Tim. 4:6), called on Timothy to be ready to carry on the work of the proclamation of the true gospel. In a letter filled with encouragement and instruction, Paul, as a mentor, called on Timothy to focus again on serving Christ and to keep on being faithful.

Interpreting the Scriptures

The Introduction (1:1–5)

Paul assured Timothy that he was constantly remembering him in his prayers "night and day" (1:3b). Paul was a prayer warrior, and this description can be easily seen in the way he assured individuals and churches that he was praying for them constantly, a trait we might do well to emulate. He talked of longing to see Timothy, for he recalled Timothy's "tears," evidently referring to the tears he saw on Timothy's face at their last parting. Paul tenderly noted that his seeing Timothy again would fill him with joy (1:4).

Immediately following the traditional greeting, Paul had referred to his own heritage of serving God with a clear conscience, a heritage he had maintained (1:3a). He reminded Timothy that Timothy too had a heritage of which he could be proud, for he too had a sincere, therefore non-hypocritical, faith that had been exercised first by his grandmother Lois and by his mother Eunice (1:5).

Re-invigorate Your Faith (1:6–8)

1:6. Paul reminded Timothy to "fan into flame the gift of God" that was in him. Paul urged Timothy to stir up his ministerial gift in much the same way that someone enjoying or utilizing fire in a fireplace would watch it constantly and fan or stoke it to keep it burning strongly. Timothy was to re-invigorate or re-awaken the fire of the Lord in him. In talking of "the laying on of my hands," Paul was obviously referring to when Timothy was ordained into the gospel ministry.

1:7. Paul pointed out that God has not given believers the spirit that is characterized by timidity but one that is characterized by power, love, and self-discipline. The power of the Holy Spirit is available to believers. However, the power must be demonstrated in love. When the power of God is displayed in an unloving manner, it becomes counter-productive. Self-discipline or a sound mind is what keeps one from behaving in an unloving manner. Care must be taken not to jump to the conclusion that Timothy had the tendency to be timid. It is possible that Paul was simply using "timidity" as the very opposite of the "power" that characterizes the spirit God gives to believers.

1:8. Paul called on Timothy not to be ashamed to testify about our Lord. Here again, this does not mean that Timothy was feeling shame on account of the gospel. Not only should Timothy boldly testify about Christ, but he should also not be ashamed of Paul. On the contrary, Timothy should be willing to suffer for the gospel in the same way that Paul was. In referring to the power of God for the second time in four verses, Paul was pointing out that even the seeming weakness of being imprisoned for the sake of the gospel ironically ended up displaying the power of God.

Remember the Foundation of Your Faith (1:9–12)

1:9–10. Paul reminded Timothy of the foundation of his faith. It is God who has saved us, and God has "saved us and called us" to lead holy lives for God's "purpose and grace." In emphasizing the grace of God, Paul reminded Timothy that our good works do not save us. Paul's doctrine of grace (God's unmerited favor) was central to his theology. Consider a few examples. In Romans, Paul said, "For we maintain that a man is justified by faith apart from observing the law" (Romans 3:28). In the following chapter he would link faith to grace, saying, "Therefore, the promise comes by faith, so that it may be by grace" (Rom. 4:16). In Ephesians he wrote, "For it is by grace you have been saved through faith—and this not from yourselves, it is the gift of God—not by works, so that no one can boast" (Ephesians 2:8–9). He told Titus, "He saved us, not because of righteous things we had done, but because of his mercy" (Titus 3:5).

This grace of God was given to us in Christ Jesus before the beginning of time, but it was not revealed until our Lord came in the flesh into this world (2 Tim. 1:9–10). In Christ's death, burial, and resurrection, our Lord "destroyed death" and through the gospel "brought life and immortality to light." Our Lord made it possible for us to envision immortality, the very opposite of death.

1:11. Paul repeated here the three nouns he had used in describing his mission in 1 Timothy 2:7—a "herald," an "apostle," and a "teacher." He was a "herald" in that he was a messenger making a public pronounce-ment of the gospel. He was an "apostle" in that Christ had sent him out as a missionary. He was a "teacher" in that he opened up the word of God for the people. In 1 Timothy 2:7 he expounded on the last of these, saying that he was appointed "a teacher of the true faith to the Gentiles."

1:12. Paul acknowledged that he was suffering, but he returned to the theme that he was not ashamed of his imprisonment and suffering. In 2 Timothy 1:8 he had exhorted Timothy that he should not be "ashamed" of testifying about our Lord. Here, he said he himself was "not ashamed." What Paul said calls to mind his statement in his Letter to the Romans, "I am not ashamed of the gospel" (Rom. 1:16a).

While in Romans 1:16 Paul had said that the reason for his not being ashamed of the gospel was that it was "the power of God for the salva-tion of everyone who believes" (Rom. 1:16b), here in 2 Timothy 1:8 he said that he was not ashamed because he knew whom he had believed. Paul was convinced that God had the ability to guard what he had entrusted to him until the last day. God is an omnipotent God, and no one and nothing can snatch anything or anyone from his hand. This echoes our Lord's statement in John 10:27–30 and Paul's own words in Romans 8:38–39.

Guard Your Faith (1:13–14)

Paul wanted Timothy to be aware that he had received "sound teaching" from Paul. Timothy was to maintain the pattern of "sound teaching" with a strong "faith," which would ensure that he would grasp the teach-ing, and with "love," which would characterize the manner in which he would teach others. He was to guard the sound teaching like a pearl of great price. However, he needed to know that he could do that only "with the help of the Holy Spirit" who lives in every believer.

Pass On Your Faith (2:1–2)

Here Paul outlined the basic structure of discipleship training. Beginning with himself, Paul lined up four generations of discipleship trainers and disciples. The discipleship trainer is to teach faithful people who in turn are to teach others, and so on.

Endure Hardship On Account of Your Faith (2:3–10)

2:3–7. Paul emphasized that Timothy must be ready to "endure hardship." Paul employed three vivid examples from everyday life. The soldier is so intent on pleasing the commanding officer that the soldier will not become entangled with "civilian affairs." The athlete is diligent to compete according to the rules; otherwise he or she cannot win. Finally, the "hardworking farmer" must be ahead of the lazy farmer in receiving a share of the crops. Timothy must be careful to be like the "good soldier," the superior athlete, and the "hardworking farmer."

2:8–10. Paul returned to the topic of his suffering. As a trailblazer, he was suffering even to the point of being chained like a common criminal, but God's word is never chained. After all, Christ's crucifixion resulted in his being raised from the dead. Similarly, Paul's suffering would lead to the salvation of souls, bringing glory that is eternal.

Be Assured of Your Faith (2:11–13)

Like a teacher who signals that the students need to note a particular point, Paul signaled that what he was about to say was "trustworthy" or very important. He had used the same expression three times in 1 Timothy (see 1 Tim. 1:15; 3:1; 4:9). Dying with or for our Lord would only precede living with our Lord, and enduring hardship for him would only precede reigning with him. We must be careful, though, for if we disown our Lord, he also will disown us. However, Christ cannot disown himself, and so even if we are faithless, he remains faithful.

Demonstrate Your Faith (2:14–15)

2:14. Paul advised Timothy to warn people against "quarrelling about words," what he elsewhere refers to as "godless chatter" (see 1 Tim. 6:20; 2 Tim. 2:16), "foolish and stupid arguments" (see 2:23), and "foolish controversies" (see Titus 3:9). He pointed out that any such argument "is of no value, and only ruins those who listen" (2 Tim. 2:14), is "unprofitable and useless" (Titus 3:9), and can only "produce quarrels" (2 Tim. 2:23).

2:15. Paul exhorted Timothy to lead his life in a way that always demonstrated his closeness to God. He should always present himself as a minister who had God's approval, was unashamed of his calling, and would always proclaim and teach the authentic gospel of Christ.

Focusing on the Meaning

The pep talk of a good coach at halftime in any sport can be very important. Teams have won or lost games depending on how effective the pep talk was. The pep talk is important irrespective of whether the team is doing well and ahead or doing poorly and behind on the scoreboard. One must bear in mind that an isolated clause from the coach's speech may or may not tell you how the team had performed in the first half of the game. For instance, suppose one of the coach's statements to encourage the players was, *Play with emotion!* The coach could be saying those words because the coach believed the players had not been playing with emotion—with sufficient intensity, focus, and excitement—and the coach was asking them to begin doing so. The coach could also be saying the statement because he or she knew the players were already playing with emotion and the coach was making sure they would continue that level of play and not relax. Finally, the coach could be saying that the players were playing with some emotion but that they needed to dig deeper and play with even more emotion. One would therefore risk being wrong by jumping to any conclusion regarding how the players had been playing if his or her only basis for the conclusion was that statement.

Second Timothy can be seen as a *pep talk* from Timothy's father-in-the-Lord, and therefore *coach*. Paul exhorted Timothy to focus again on serving Christ or to keep on focusing on serving Christ and to keep on being faithful.

How about you? When you see the exhortation to keep on being faithful, does it say to you that you need to begin to be faithful, or is it saying that you need to continue to be as faithful as you are now, or is it saying that you need to be even more faithful than you are now? What encouragement do you need to move on with the right spiritual intensity?

TEACHING PLANS

Teaching Plan—Varied Learning Activities

Connect with Life

1. Prior to class, create a paper with a form on it and make copies for each person. The form should look something like the illustration titled, "How Awake Are You?" (A copy is available in "Teaching Resource Items" for this study at www.baptistwaypress.org.)

How Awake Are You?	
When you wake up, what does it take to get you going?	
What does it take to wake you up spiritually?	
Do you wake up every day and choose to serve Christ, or do you go for longer periods of time before you serve?	
When you serve Christ, how do you serve Christ?	

2. Distribute the sheets to learners as they enter the room; offer pens and pencils if needed. Ask them to fill in their answers and then discuss the answers with two or three people near them.

3. After giving your class some time to discuss their answers, read the questions and invite participants to share their answers. Be prepared to answer for yourself, especially if there are no answers from the class.

4. Explain that this lesson is about Paul's call to Timothy to re-awaken to serving Christ. Point out that this encouragement was not just for

Timothy, but the message extends to all Christians, including your class. Have someone lead the class in prayer.

Guide Bible Study

5. Bring pictures of a soldier, a bat (or a ball or an athlete), and a hoe (or other farm implement) to class. Divide the class in three small groups or more as long as the groups are in multiples of three (three, six, or nine groups, etc.). Aim for no more than six members in each group. Have enough sets of the three pictures so that each group will get one item from each set.

6. Call for someone from each group to select one of the three items. Tell each group they are either soldiers, athletes, or farmers based on their chosen item.

7. Create three columns on a white board or poster board with the headings: "Soldier," "Athlete," and "Farmer."

8. Tell the groups to think about characteristics attributed to their profession as the lesson's passages are read, raising their hand as they think of one. Read 2 Timothy 1:6–14 and then 2:1–15 verse by verse, stopping between verses for responses. Record the attributes in the columns. (For example, in 2 Timothy 1:8 Paul asked Timothy to share with him in his suffering for the gospel. Soldiers, athletes, and farmers are all willing to suffer in their work.)

9. After recording all attributes, discuss those that Paul was asking Timothy to display (courage, willingness to suffer, etc). Lead the class to consider whether Christians today should be willing to display these attributes.

10. Ask, *How awake are soldiers, athletes, and farmers to their cause?* Follow with, *How awake are you to your cause of faith and service to Christ?*

11. Summarize the lesson's content, highlighting the main points not already discussed.

Encourage Application

12. Enlist someone to read aloud the small article, "Guard," in the *Study Guide*. Have the small groups discuss their thoughts on the reading. Then have them discuss whether they are being faithful by being a disciple who is leading others to be disciples.

13. Refer to the questions at the end of the lesson in the *Study Guide*, and ask the small groups to read, answer, and discuss each question. If time is limited, instruct the groups to focus on question 1, "What is another way to say, 'fan into flame the gift of God' (1:6)? How can you do that in your life? How can you encourage others to ignite their faith?"

14. Challenge your members to consider in the coming week the attributes Paul asked Timothy to display and the attributes Christians should display. Ask them to think about soldiers, athletes, and farmers. Pointing to some of the attributes listed on the board, challenge them to wake up daily and make a decision to serve Christ faithfully with those characteristics. You may want to add some attributes that the class did not mention (for example a few important ones are courage, power, love, discipline, willingness to suffer, diligence, etc.)

15. Invite final thoughts, and add your own. Close in prayer.

Teaching Plan—Lecture and Questions

Connect with Life

1. Prior to class, display these questions:
   - What does it take to wake you up in the morning?
   - What does it take to wake you up to faithfully serving Christ?
   - Do you wake up every day to faithfully serving Christ?

2. Read the questions aloud one at a time, calling for answers to each before moving to the next.

3. Now ask, *Why do we sometimes choose to not stay awake, to not stay active to serving God?* Point out that the final section, "Implications

and Actions," in the lesson in the *Study Guide* has some answers listed. Review them, and encourage the class to be prepared to give some of their own answers.

4. Explain that in this lesson the class will be looking at Paul's challenge to Timothy on this subject, awakening to serving Christ again. Invite someone to lead in prayer.

Guide Bible Study

5. Distribute notepaper and a pen or pencil to each person.

6. Point out that at the time Paul wrote this final letter to Timothy, Paul evidently expected to die soon for faithfully serving God.

7. Call for someone to read 2 Timothy 1:6–7. Summarize the *Study Guide* section, "Wake Up Your Faith in Christ (1:6–7)." Add insights on these verses from "Bible Comments" in this *Teaching Guide*. Refer to verse 7, and ask, *Does your service to Christ show more fear or more power, love, and sound mind (self-discipline)?*

8. Point out that Paul might have thought that Timothy might be afraid to share his faith, and so he gave Timothy, and all Christians, some reasons to stand strong. Ask the class to note (on the paper provided earlier) those reasons as someone reads verses 8–14. Ask the class what they noted as they listened. Also mention the three reasons listed in the *Study Guide* section, "Keep Going Despite Difficulties (1:8–12)."

9. Enlist someone to read 2 Timothy 2:1–15. Before the reading, instruct members to note (on the paper provided earlier) during the reading of the Scripture the actions Paul was asking Timothy to take. For instance, in the first few verses, Paul told him to "be strong," "entrust," and "endure." Ask members to name what they noted.

10. Ask, *How many of these actions do you display as you serve Christ?* Now point out that Paul was asking Timothy, and us, to do these things by relying on God, not ourselves (2 Tim. 2:1).

11. Summarize the *Study Guide* section, "Keep Living and Serving with Disciplined Purpose (2:1–15)," and add insights from "Bible Comments" on these verses in this *Teaching Guide.*

Encourage Application

12. Summarize or read the concluding section, "Implications and Actions," in the lesson in the *Study Guide*. Tie this section back to the discussion at the beginning of the class when you talked about reasons for not serving God faithfully and daily (see step 3). Ask, *How can we get rid of the excuses that keep us from serving Christ daily, faithfully, and with everything we have?*

13. Prior to class, post the four bullet points from the small article, "Passing the Deposit Along," in the *Study Guide.*
    - To your children or grandchildren? To other children in your life?
    - In your church?
    - In your community?
    - At work or school?

14. Call for someone to read the small article, "Guard," in the *Study Guide* lesson.

15. Point to the posted questions, and ask, *How can we awaken daily and serve God by passing on God's story to each of these groups?*

16. Challenge your class to take action on their answers during the coming week. Close in prayer.

NOTES ———————————————————————————

1. Unless otherwise indicated, all Scripture quotations in lessons 5–7 and 12–13 are from the New International Version, 1984 edition.

FOCAL TEXT
2 Timothy 4:1–8, 16–18

BACKGROUND
2 Timothy 4

MAIN IDEA
As Paul called Timothy to continued faithful service, Paul testified of a future filled with hope.

QUESTION TO EXPLORE
What can we do when we are discouraged or otherwise question the value of living in faithfulness to God?

TEACHING AIM
To lead adults to testify of their experiences of God's care in difficult times and what these experiences mean to them

LESSON THIRTEEN
Toward a Future Filled with Hope

BIBLE COMMENTS

Understanding the Context

In 2 Timothy, Paul was leaving his legacy to the young pastor, Timothy, whom he was proud to call his "son" (2 Timothy 1:2). He was leaving his legacy not as someone who was on his deathbed but as someone who knew his days were winding down.

Paul focused on encouragement and on instruction. The encouragement was two-pronged. Sometimes Paul was encouraging Timothy. At other times Paul was asking him to continue to encourage others. The instruction too was two-pronged. At times Paul was exhorting Timothy not to deviate from the sound doctrine that he had been taught, while at other times he was exhorting him to continue to proclaim and teach the same sound doctrine.

Paul reminded Timothy of how he (Timothy) had closely followed his teaching, conduct, aim, faith, patience, love, steadfastness, persecutions, and sufferings (2 Tim. 3:10–11). Obviously Timothy, who was Paul's associate and disciple, knew Paul and his ministry very well, and vice versa.

Paul talked of his suffering several times in this letter (see 1:8–12; 2:10; 3:11; 4:14, 16). Paul's suffering was something no one can dismiss. However, he did not find it strange that he was suffering for the sake of the gospel of Christ. In fact, he said, "Everyone who wants to live a godly life in Christ Jesus will be persecuted" (3:12).

Paul exhorted Timothy to continue to adhere to the sound doctrine he had received, for Timothy knew the people from whom he had learned it. Paul reminded Timothy of the fact that he had known the Holy Scriptures "from infancy" (3:15), a reference to the godly heritage Timothy had, having had a grandmother and a mother who were both godly women (see 1:5; 3:14–15).

Paul then talked of the immeasurable value of Scripture as he declared that all Scripture is "God-breathed" (or inspired by God) and is profitable (3:16). It is profitable "for teaching, rebuking, correcting and training in righteousness" (3:16). The Scripture is therefore an invaluable tool to get the servant of God "thoroughly equipped for every good work" (3:17). Paul exhorted and appealed to Timothy, who was armed with this sound doctrine, to keep on ministering, for in the final analysis victory is assured.

Interpreting the Scriptures

The Charge to Preach (4:1–2)

4:1. Paul gave Timothy a solemn "charge" to preach. In emphasizing the solemnity of the charge, he invoked "the presence of God and of Christ Jesus, who will judge the living and the dead." The reference to the judgment by Christ echoes what Paul had said in 2 Corinthians: "For we must all appear before the judgment seat of Christ, that each one may receive what is due him for the things done while in the body, whether good or bad" (2 Corinthians 5:10). Paul added in 2 Timothy 4:1, "in view of his appearing and his kingdom," thus referring to the Second Coming of Christ (see 1 Thessalonians 4:13–18).

4:2. Paul charged Timothy with five commands. First, he was to "preach the Word," or to *keep on preaching the Word*. The "Word" must be the Word of God, not that of human beings. Next, he said, "be prepared in season and out of season." The minister of God must be ready at all times, when it is convenient and when it is not. The next two commands are, "correct, rebuke." The command to "correct" people is the exhortation to bring errors to light, to expose, and to convict or convince the one making the mistake. The command to "rebuke" people is the exhortation to censure or admonish the person. Obviously, people do not readily welcome being corrected, let alone rebuked. The final command in this charge is to "encourage." This command is for Timothy to exhort, appeal to, or comfort the person. Paul would add that all of this must be done "with great patience and careful instruction." In fulfilling the charge, Timothy must have the right attitude—being patient with the people—and the content of his teaching must always be sound. Timothy needed to be ready to combat the false teaching that was rampant in Ephesus. Actually, every minister needs to be so ready.

The Response to Expect (4:3–4)

4:3. Paul told Timothy not to expect that most of the people he would deal with would have eager listening ears. On the contrary, he said, people would hate "sound doctrine." They would have "itching ears," wanting to hear only what would soothe their ears, and they would have no lack of teachers who would tell them exactly what they would like to hear.

4:4. People would actually abandon the truth and embrace "myths" wherever they could find them, even though resorting to myths would result in nothing but deceit, frustration, and disappointment.

The Charge to Keep Ministering (4:5)

Even though many people would be seeking false teaching and there would be no lack of teachers who would satisfy them, Timothy must keep four things in mind. He must "keep [his] head in all situations." He was saying that Timothy must be sure that he had a clear mind, in other words, that he must think clearly or *keep his cool* at all times and in all situations. Timothy was also to "endure hardship." Here Paul returned to the theme of suffering for the sake of the gospel of Christ (see 1 Timothy 1:8, 12; 2:3; 3:11–12). Timothy must also "do the work of an evangelist." Timothy's work of an evangelist was to complement his ministry as a preacher. He was to make sure he was pointing people to Christ.

The Example of Paul (4:6–8)

4:6. Paul said that he was "already being poured out like a drink offering." In Philippians 2:17 Paul had said, "But even if I am being poured out like a drink offering on the sacrifice and service coming from your faith. . . ." The reference to being "poured out like a drink offering" conjures up the image in the Old Testament of wine that was poured in sacrifice to God (for example, see Exodus 29:40–41; Leviticus 23:13; Numbers 15:4–10; 28:7). The difference between "*even if I am* being poured out" (italics added for emphasis) in the Philippians passage and the "*I am already* being poured out" (italics added for emphasis) in 2 Timothy 4:6 is noteworthy. Whereas when Paul wrote Philippians he was anticipating release from his first imprisonment in Rome, his words in Second Timothy suggest that he was not expecting to be released from this his second imprisonment in Rome.

Paul would add, "and the time has come for my departure." This clause can be variously translated, *and the time for my departure is imminent, and the time of my departure is near,* or "and the time of my departure is at hand" (KJV). In light of these other possible renderings, the conclusion that is sometimes drawn here that Paul wrote this letter practically from his *deathbed* is a bit of an overstatement. Paul urged Timothy to endeavor to come to see him "before winter" (2 Tim. 4:21). He also asked Timothy to bring with him John Mark, his scrolls, and the cloak he had left with Carpus at Troas (see 4:11–13). These requests meant that he was expecting to live to see the following winter. Paul believed that the time for him to leave this earth was near, but he did not believe that it was going to be a matter of weeks, let alone days or hours.

4:7. Paul made three key declarations here. In the first of these he said, "I have fought the good fight." Some scholars contend that the picture here is a military one, while others contend that it is athletic, such as boxing. Actually, there is no reason it cannot be both. The force of the illustration is not lost either way. In the second he declared, "I have finished the race." The picture here is obviously athletic, conjuring up the image of an athlete who does not just run part of the course but who actually gets to the finish line. Finally, Paul declared, "I have kept the faith." Any attempt to make this also into an athletic illustration to make it mean "I have followed the rules" is forced. "Faith" here has to mean what Paul always calls—actually, what the Bible everywhere calls—faith. He was simply but emphatically saying, *I have remained faithful to God.*

4:8. Paul was saying here that he had already won the victory. All that was left was the award ceremony. The "crown of righteousness" awaited him, and the Lord who is "the righteous judge" would give him that award on the day of judgment. Paul then made sure neither Timothy nor anyone else misunderstood him as saying that the crown he was talking of awaited him alone. This crown awaits every believer. He would therefore add, "and not only to me, but also to all those who have longed for his appearing."

The Faithfulness of the Lord (4:16–18)

4:16. Paul told Timothy that at his "first defense" no one had come to his support and that everyone had deserted him. His talking of his "first defense" may mean he was anticipating a second defense. Church tradition indicates that Paul was released from his first imprisonment in Rome but was imprisoned again later, an imprisonment that would eventually end in his being beheaded for the sake of the gospel. Paul expressed forgiveness for those who had deserted him, as he said, "May it not be held against them."

4:17. While human beings deserted him, the ever-faithful Lord did not. Instead, the Lord stood by him and strengthened Paul so that he could proclaim the gospel to the Gentiles. In talking of his being "delivered from the lion's mouth," he was most likely talking of being *delivered from the hand of the Roman emperor* or from some serious danger that Paul did not go into.

4:18. Paul expressed confidence that the Lord would rescue him "from every evil attack." He could be saying that the three obviously non-exhaustive examples of rescue he had referred to—rescue from the great harm intended by Alexander the metalworker (4:14–15), rescue in spite of the fact that his own people had deserted him (4:16), and rescue from the lion's mouth (4:17)—were strong indications that the Lord would rescue him from any evil attack that is out there.

Paul could not help but add a doxology, "To him be glory for ever and ever. Amen."

Focusing on the Meaning

Very few good things in life come easily. In fact, you would be hard pressed to come up with one. I found that out as a young boy growing up. When I was eight years old, my immediate younger brother, Fortune, who was six then, and I were each learning how to ride a bicycle. One day, I fell while learning to ride, and I scraped my knee. That was enough to get me to stop learning. Fortune, however, continued to learn, and a short time later he was riding his bicycle everywhere and was even able to give adults a ride. Some of my peers started teasing me that my younger brother could ride a bicycle, while I could not. It took the teasing for me to get my determination back. I resumed learning how to ride a bicycle, and shortly afterwards I too was riding my bicycle everywhere. Two years later, I went to live with my uncle in another town. The people of that town were so impressed at how I rode my bicycle like an adult that they nicknamed me *the biker.* I discovered that the scrapes I had had on my knee while learning were worth it after all.

One of the fascinating stories of the London Olympics in 2012 was that of Gabby Douglas. Gabby was so interested in gymnastics that as a little girl she got the blessing and support of her parents to go out-of-state to live with another family so she could learn to be a good gymnast. She got so good that she won the gold medal in the Women's All-around at the London Olympics. Her sacrifice and that of her family had paid off.[1]

Paul's advice to Timothy was a rephrasing of what he had said in other letters. In Galatians 6:9 Paul said, "Let us not become weary in doing good, for at the proper time we will reap a harvest, if we do not give up." In Romans 8:18 Paul said, "I consider that our present sufferings are not worth comparing with the glory that will be revealed in us."

Paul's advice was good for Timothy, and it is good for you and me. We should always remember that the eternal crown of glory that clearly awaits us in heaven far outweighs any suffering for Christ here on earth.

TEACHING PLANS

Teaching Plan—Varied Learning Activities

Connect with Life

1. Ask members to define what *hope* might mean to someone who is not a Christian and then to someone who is. For example, it might mean *blind, wishful thinking* to a non-Christian and *believing that God will live up to his promises* to a Christian. Prior to class, look up the definition from a secular dictionary (such as Merriam-Webster)

and one from a Bible dictionary (such as Easton's), and read the definitions aloud to the class.

2. Referring to the world's view, ask members to come up with some sentences using hope. Give the examples, *I hope to get into that college,* and *My seven-year old son hopes to be a rich and famous football player someday.* After a few answers, call for sentences using the word from a Christian view. Give the example, *My hope is in trusting that my God will see me through this time in my life.* Be ready with examples of your own for both of these.

3. Explain that this lesson comes from the final letter written by Paul to Timothy. At the time of writing, Paul felt his life was drawing to a close, and yet he was excited to share his testimony of hope despite his situation. Paul's letter challenged Timothy to spread the news of Christ by encouraging him with the kind of hope that does not come from the world but comes only from God.

4. Say, *As we study this chapter, be alert to what it may say to you about being faithful to God and sharing God's message in your own difficult times.* Invite someone to lead in prayer.

Guide Bible Study

5. Prior to the class session, enlist someone to dramatically read 2 Timothy 4:1–8; 16–18, acting as if writing the letter. Give the person time to prepare fully. Invite the person to dress as Paul or to add to the scene in other ways if he or she chooses.

6. After the reading, ask the class the questions from near the end of the lesson in the *Study Guide.*

7. Summarize the *Study Guide* section, "Hope in the Presence of God (4:1–5)," especially highlighting the five realities discussed as well as Paul's five commands that bring Christians hope.

8. Summarize the section, "Hope That Finishes Well (4:6–8)," pointing out the imagery Paul used, referring to his impending death. Add insights on 2 Timothy 4:6–8 from "Bible Comments" in this *Teaching Guide.* Ask, *If you knew you were dying, how well do you think your thoughts would match Paul's in these verses? What place*

would spreading God's story and encouraging others to spread God's story have in your mind?

9. Summarize the section, "Hope in the Heavenly Kingdom (4:16–18)." Add insights on these verses from "Bible Comments" in this *Teaching Guide*.

Encourage Application

10. Form the class into small groups of no more than six people each. Instruct group members to share with each other the following:
    - Times when either they or someone they know has gone through hard times but kept their hope in Christ
    - Whether the hard times were a result of living a faithful life to Christ
    - Ways they saw God's love and care during that time

    (A copy of these group instructions is available in "Teaching Resource Items" for this study at www.baptistwaypress.org.)

11. Make available a blank index card and a pen or pencil to each member. Keeping the same groups as in step 10, have group members name Scripture that speaks to the hope that comes only from God. Have each member write the verses on their card. Examples are
    - "I can do everything through him who strengthens me" (Philippians 4:13).
    - "For to me, to live is Christ and to die is gain" (Phil. 1:21).
    - "You intended to harm me, but God intended it for good to accomplish what is now being done . . . " (Genesis 50:20).
    - "Now to him who is able to do immeasurably more than all we ask or imagine . . . " (Ephesians 3:20).

12. Challenge members to be alert to give their Scripture cards to someone who needs encouragement during the week, as Paul gave his letter to Timothy. Challenge them to share their stories of hope in Christ by telling others of the ways God loved and cared for them during their trials past or present. Close in prayer.

Teaching Plan—Lecture and Questions

Connect with Life

1. Post the following Scripture references: "Psalm 42:11"; "Psalm 71:5"; and "1 Peter 1:3." Enlist two people with different translations to find and read each verse. Discuss each verse's meaning based on the two translations. Ask what word or idea ties the verses together (hope).

2. Refer to and summarize the ideas about hope in the introduction to the lesson in the *Study Guide.*

3. Call for examples of people who have dealt with traumatic situations and yet held their hope in Christ. Ask, *What in their behavior showed this hope?*

4. Tell the class that in this lesson on 2 Timothy 4 they will see Paul's continued hope in Christ, the type of hope that comes only from God, despite having to experience difficulties and also knowing he would soon die because of his faithful service to Christ. Have someone lead the class in prayer.

Guide Bible Study

5. From the section, "Hope in the Presence of God (4:1–5)," in the *Study Guide* lesson, highlight the five realities and the five commands.

6. Enlist two people to read Scripture. One is to read 2 Timothy 4:1–5 from the Scripture printed in the *Study Guide* (NIV84), and the other is to read the same passage from the New American Standard Bible if available (or another translation). Tell your class to listen for the advice Paul gave Timothy, and all Christians, by noting the verbs, paying special attention to verses 2 and 5. Call for the reading of 2 Timothy 4:1–5 from each translation. Ask what instructions the class noted (preach, be prepared, correct, rebuke, encourage, keep your head, endure, do the work of an evangelist, discharge all duties). List answers on a markerboard, noting the slight difference in the wording of each translation.

7. Lead the class to look at the list and describe a life lived according to these instructions. From the questions at the end of the lesson in the *Study Guide,* ask question 2, "How well do you 'keep your head' in difficult times (2 Tim. 4:5)? What can we do to increase the possibility of our doing that?"

8. Have someone read 4:6–8. Summarize the *Study Guide* section, "Hope that Finishes Well (4:6–8)." Add insights on 2 Timothy 4:6–8 from "Bible Comments" in this *Teaching Guide.* From the questions in the lesson in the *Study Guide,* ask, "Consider the meaning of "departure" in 2 Timothy 4:6. How do you see this passage as being helpful to someone dealing with his or her own approaching death or the death of a loved one?"

9. Enlist someone to read 4:16–18. Summarize the *Study Guide* section, "Hope in the Heavenly Kingdom (4:16–18)." Add insights on 2 Timothy 4:16–18 from "Bible Comments" in this *Teaching Guide.* From the questions in the *Study Guide,* ask, "Which of these two encourages you more in your faith: (1) living faithfully now in the kingdom of heaven or (2) looking with faith toward the heavenly kingdom?"

Encourage Application

10. Use information in "Implications and Actions" in the *Study Guide* and in "Focusing on the Meaning" in this *Teaching Guide* to help participants apply the lesson to their lives.

11. Invite members to share stories of when they felt God's love and care during hard times. Ask what that meant to them. Challenge members to share their stories of God's love with people who are going through trials, just as Paul did with Timothy. Close in prayer.

NOTES

1. http://www.biography.com/people/gabby-douglas-20900057?page=1. Accessed 3/19/14.

How to Order More Bible Study Materials

It's easy! Just fill in the following information. For additional Bible study materials available both in print and online, see www.baptistwaypress.org, or get a complete order form of available print materials—including Spanish materials—by calling 1-866-249-1799 or e-mailing baptistway@texasbaptists.org.

Title of item	Price	Quantity	Cost
This Issue:			
Letters to the Ephesians and Timothy—Study Guide (BWP001182)	$3.95	_____	_____
Letters to the Ephesians and Timothy—Large Print Study Guide (BWP001183)	$4.25	_____	_____
Letters to the Ephesians and Timothy—Teaching Guide (BWP001184)	$4.95	_____	_____
Additional Issues Available:			
14 Habits of Highly Effective Disciples—Study Guide (BWP001177)	$3.95	_____	_____
14 Habits of Highly Effective Disciples—Large Print Study Guide (BWP001178)	$4.25	_____	_____
14 Habits of Highly Effective Disciples—Teaching Guide (BWP001179)	$4.95	_____	_____
Growing Together in Christ—Study Guide (BWP001036)	$3.25	_____	_____
Growing Together in Christ—Teaching Guide (BWP001038)	$3.75	_____	_____
Guidance for the Seasons of Life—Study Guide (BWP001157)	$3.95	_____	_____
Guidance for the Seasons of Life—Large Print Study Guide (BWP001158)	$4.25	_____	_____
Guidance for the Seasons of Life—Teaching Guide (BWP001159)	$4.95	_____	_____
Living Generously for Jesus' Sake—Study Guide (BWP001137)	$3.95	_____	_____
Living Generously for Jesus' Sake—Large Print Study Guide (BWP001138)	$4.25	_____	_____
Living Generously for Jesus' Sake—Teaching Guide (BWP001139)	$4.95	_____	_____
Living Faith in Daily Life—Study Guide (BWP001095)	$3.55	_____	_____
Living Faith in Daily Life—Large Print Study Guide (BWP001096)	$3.95	_____	_____
Living Faith in Daily Life—Teaching Guide (BWP001097)	$4.25	_____	_____
Participating in God's Mission—Study Guide (BWP001077)	$3.55	_____	_____
Participating in God's Mission—Large Print Study Guide (BWP001078)	$3.95	_____	_____
Participating in God's Mission—Teaching Guide (BWP001079)	$3.95	_____	_____
Profiles in Character—Study Guide (BWP001112)	$3.55	_____	_____
Profiles in Character—Large Print Study Guide (BWP001113)	$4.25	_____	_____
Profiles in Character—Teaching Guide (BWP001114)	$4.95	_____	_____
Genesis: People Relating to God—Study Guide (BWP001088)	$2.35	_____	_____
Genesis: People Relating to God—Large Print Study Guide (BWP001089)	$2.75	_____	_____
Genesis: People Relating to God—Teaching Guide (BWP001090)	$2.95	_____	_____
Ezra, Haggai, Zechariah, Nehemiah, Malachi—Study Guide (BWP001071)	$3.25	_____	_____
Ezra, Haggai, Zechariah, Nehemiah, Malachi—Large Print Study Guide (BWP001072)	$3.55	_____	_____
Ezra, Haggai, Zechariah, Nehemiah, Malachi—Teaching Guide (BWP001073)	$3.75	_____	_____
Psalms: Songs from the Heart of Faith—Study Guide (BWP001152)	$3.95	_____	_____
Psalms: Songs from the Heart of Faith—Large Print Study Guide (BWP001153)	$4.25	_____	_____
Psalms: Songs from the Heart of Faith—Teaching Guide (BWP001154)	$4.95	_____	_____
Jeremiah and Ezekiel: Prophets of Judgment and Hope—Study Guide (BWP001172)	$3.95	_____	_____
Jeremiah and Ezekiel: Prophets of Judgment and Hope—Large Print Study Guide (BWP001173)	$4.25	_____	_____
Jeremiah and Ezekiel: Prophets of Judgment and Hope—Teaching Guide (BWP001174)	$4.95	_____	_____
Amos. Hosea, Isaiah, Micah: Calling for Justice, Mercy, and Faithfulness—Study Guide (BWP001132)	$3.95	_____	_____
Amos. Hosea, Isaiah, Micah: Calling for Justice, Mercy, and Faithfulness—Large Print Study Guide (BWP001133)	$4.25	_____	_____
Amos. Hosea, Isaiah, Micah: Calling for Justice, Mercy, and Faithfulness—Teaching Guide (BWP001134)	$4.95	_____	_____
The Gospel of Matthew: A Primer for Discipleship—Study Guide (BWP001127)	$3.95	_____	_____
The Gospel of Matthew: A Primer for Discipleship—Large Print Study Guide (BWP001128)	$4.25	_____	_____
The Gospel of Matthew: A Primer for Discipleship—Teaching Guide (BWP001129)	$4.95	_____	_____
The Gospel of Mark: People Responding to Jesus—Study Guide (BWP001147)	$3.95	_____	_____
The Gospel of Mark: People Responding to Jesus—Large Print Study Guide (BWP001148)	$4.25	_____	_____
The Gospel of Mark: People Responding to Jesus—Teaching Guide (BWP001149)	$4.95	_____	_____
The Gospel of Luke: Jesus' Personal Touch—Study Guide (BWP001167)	$3.95	_____	_____
The Gospel of Luke: Jesus' Personal Touch—Large Print Study Guide (BWP001168)	$4.25	_____	_____
The Gospel of Luke: Jesus' Personal Touch—Teaching Guide (BWP001169)	$4.95	_____	_____
The Gospel of John: Light Overcoming Darkness, Part One—Study Guide (BWP001104)	$3.55	_____	_____
The Gospel of John: Light Overcoming Darkness, Part One—Large Print Study Guide (BWP001105)	$3.95	_____	_____
The Gospel of John: Light Overcoming Darkness, Part One—Teaching Guide (BWP001106)	$4.50	_____	_____

Item	Price		
The Gospel of John: Light Overcoming Darkness, Part Two—Study Guide (BWP001109)	$3.55	_____	_____
The Gospel of John: Light Overcoming Darkness, Part Two—Large Print Study Guide (BWP001110)	$3.95	_____	_____
The Gospel of John: Light Overcoming Darkness, Part Two—Teaching Guide (BWP001111)	$4.50	_____	_____
The Book of Acts: Time to Act on Acts 1:8—Study Guide (BWP001142)	$3.95	_____	_____
The Book of Acts: Time to Act on Acts 1:8—Large Print Study Guide (BWP001143)	$4.25	_____	_____
The Book of Acts: Time to Act on Acts 1:8—Teaching Guide (BWP001144)	$4.95	_____	_____
The Corinthian Letters—Study Guide (BWP001121)	$3.55	_____	_____
The Corinthian Letters—Large Print Study Guide (BWP001122)	$4.25	_____	_____
The Corinthian Letters—Teaching Guide (BWP001123)	$4.95	_____	_____
Galatians and 1&2 Thessalonians—Study Guide (BWP001080)	$3.55	_____	_____
Galatians and 1&2 Thessalonians—Large Print Study Guide (BWP001081)	$3.95	_____	_____
Galatians and 1&2 Thessalonians—Teaching Guide (BWP001082)	$3.95	_____	_____
Hebrews and the Letters of Peter—Study Guide (BWP001162)	$3.95	_____	_____
Hebrews and the Letters of Peter—Large Print Study Guide (BWP001163)	$4.25	_____	_____
Hebrews and the Letters of Peter—Teaching Guide (BWP001164)	$4.95	_____	_____
Letters of James and John—Study Guide (BWP001101)	$3.55	_____	_____
Letters of James and John—Large Print Study Guide (BWP001102)	$3.95	_____	_____
Letters of James and John—Teaching Guide (BWP001103)	$4.25	_____	_____

Coming for use beginning December 2014

Item	Price		
The Gospel of John: Believe in Jesus and Live!—Study Guide (BWP001187)	$3.95	_____	_____
The Gospel of John: Believe in Jesus and Live!—Large Print Study Guide (BWP001188)	$4.25	_____	_____
The Gospel of John: Believe in Jesus and Live!—Teaching Guide (BWP001189)	$4.95	_____	_____

Standard (UPS/Mail) Shipping Charges*					
Order Value	Shipping charge**	Order Value	Shipping charge**		
$.01—$9.99	$6.50	$160.00—$199.99	$24.00		
$10.00—$19.99	$8.50	$200.00—$249.99	$28.00		
$20.00—$39.99	$9.50	$250.00—$299.99	$30.00		
$40.00—$59.99	$10.50	$300.00—$349.99	$34.00		
$60.00—$79.99	$11.50	$350.00—$399.99	$42.00		
$80.00—$99.99	$12.50	$400.00—$499.99	$50.00		
$100.00—$129.99	$15.00	$500.00—$599.99	$60.00		
$130.00—$159.99	$20.00	$600.00—$799.99	$72.00**		

Cost
of items (Order value)   _____

Shipping charges
(see chart*)   _____

TOTAL   _____

*Please call 1-866-249-1799 if the exact amount is needed prior to ordering.

**For order values $800.00 and above, please call 1-866-249-1799 or check www.baptistwaypress.org

Please allow three weeks for standard delivery. For express shipping service: Call 1-866-249-1799 for information on additional charges.

YOUR NAME

PHONE

YOUR CHURCH

DATE ORDERED

SHIPPING ADDRESS

CITY

STATE   ZIP CODE

E-MAIL

MAIL this form with your check for the total amount to:
BAPTISTWAY PRESS, Baptist General Convention of Texas,
333 North Washington, Dallas, TX 75246-1798
(Make checks to "BaptistWay Press")

OR, **CALL** your order toll-free: 1-866-249-1799
(M-Fri 8:30 a.m.-5:00 p.m. central time).

OR, **E-MAIL** your order to: baptistway@texasbaptists.org.

OR, **ORDER ONLINE** at www.baptistwaypress.org.

We look forward to receiving your order! Thank you!